Do This.
GET RICH.

Praise for the Book and its Author

"Jim Britt's insights into the psychology of wealth will give you the focus, clarity, and purpose to refine your financial plan and make the right choices for your business, your finances, and your life."

Anthony Robbins

Author, *Awaken the Giant Within and Unlimited Power*

"You can choose your own destiny or take what life gives you. Jim Britt offers 'hands on' strategies with penetrating clarity that will show you how to take control of your own financial destiny and reach your most ambitious goals."

Jay Levinson

Author, *Guerrilla Marketing Series*

"They say that 'success leaves clues.' After reading this book you'll know what those clues are and how to use them. You will want to keep it near you for quick reference. You will likely want to read it again and again on your way to success."

T. Harv Eker

Author, *Secrets of the Millionaire Mind*

"Jim Britt has been a friend and business associate for over 30 years. His work as a success coach, trainer and entrepreneur is remarkable. If you are interested in greater success, this book tells it all."

Jim Rohn

Author, *7 Strategies for Wealth & Happiness*

Do This. GET RICH.

12 things you can do now to gain financial freedom

JIM BRITT

BLUEJAY

Bluejay Book Pvt. Ltd
A-8/76, 1st Floor
Sector 16, Rohini
Delhi 110 085
info@bluejaybooksindia.com

First published in India by
Bluejay Books Pvt. Ltd. in 2014

First Published by
Square One Publishers, USA

By arrangement with
Square One Publishers, USA

This edition is for sale in India only

Printed and bound in India

Contents

To Free Enterprise—
the more enterprising you become
the freer you become.

And to my six sons, Jeff, Jim, Warren, Weston,
Will and Walker whose entrepreneurial spirit have
always been an inspiration to me.

And to my wife Joanna
whose dedication to me and to the education
of our sons has shaped all our their lives.

Foreword

Jim Britt is not a person you would expect to be a superstar in the business of success and personal development training. He has no college or university degree. In fact, he does not even have a high school diploma. He is not a brilliant theoretician, nor is he a natural entertainer. But today in North America, when it comes to small business success counseling, he is at the top. Why has he made such a deep and profound mark on so many lives? The answer is that *he has lived what he teaches.*

All of Jim's writing, seminars, counseling, and training are based on his personal experience. His childhood was humble. His first jobs doing menial labor taught him the value of attitude, striving always to do his best. His first job in sales taught him the value of time management and of customer service. He struggled to learn public speaking. Now training and speaking to large groups has put Jim in front of more than one million people.

Several years ago, Jim did a success counseling seminar for over one thousand people in my company, Peak Potentials. I now know from personal experience how effective he makes his presentations. I still hear references to that seminar from those in my organization.

Now in *Do This. Get Rich!*, Jim lays out his strategies for creating personal success and financial freedom for the small and home business entrepreneur. They say that "success leaves clues." After reading this book, you'll know what those clues are and how to use them to start, run, and profit from your own business. You will probably want to keep this book near your elbow for quick reference, to read again and again on your way to success.

—T. Harv Eker
The New York Times best-selling author
of *Secrets of the Millionaire Mind*

DO THIS. GET RICH!

Introduction

Money is an uncomfortable subject for most of us. We have a love affair with money and at the same time we fear it. We can't live without it and we can't live with it. Most people would rather talk about their sex lives than money. Depending on how you relate to money, it can bring great joy into your life or it can make you miserable. Money influences every area of our lives—our professions, our families, our recreation and leisure time, our home, our lifestyle, even our spiritual pursuits. Almost everything we do, every decision we make, is influenced by money.

There are five ways to have more money:

1. *Clear up your debt.*

This approach usually fails, because clearing your debt takes money, doesn't it? An all too familiar "catch-22" . . .

2. *Spend less.*

But in order to spend less, most people would have to clear up their debt. And of course, this approach usually ends in failure because to clear debt takes what? More money.

3. *Invest.*

In order to invest, what do you need? More money, right? And in order to have money to invest, you need to clear up some debt. And of course, to clear debt you need . . . more money.

4. *Earn more.*
The problem with this approach is that most people have been conditioned to believe that they are earning as much as they can based upon their current expertise or education. They would like to learn a new talent that might earn them more, but the problem is that this takes time . . . and of course, more money.

5. *Change your "relationship" with money.*
This is the one we focus on in this book. While most people feel powerless when it comes to having money, the truth is that most people give their power away to frustration, doubt, worry, and a host of other fears. The only way to have more is to change how we view money and to change our relationship with money.

In order to *have* more money in your life, you have to *do* something different. And in order to *do* something different, you have to first *know* something different can be done. And in order to *know* something different can be done, you have to first *suspect* that your present method needs improving. It has to become painfully obvious that change is definitely required. And lastly, you have to be *open* for a better way—a new approach to making money.

THE STREAMS OF EXPERIENCE

The book flows from two separate streams of experience in my own background. The first is personal; the second, professional.

I developed a solid work ethic at an early age. My family—mother, father, two sisters, and one brother—worked in the cotton fields in Oklahoma. In the summer, we would "chop cotton," cutting the weeds out that could potentially smother the crop. In the fall, we would pick cotton. Chopping cotton was hot, grueling, back-breaking work, and for very little money. The only thing harder was picking cotton. We earned a flat rate of two cents a pound (and cotton weighs very little). Needless to say, we didn't make much money, but we did learn how to work hard.

There were two valuable lessons I learned from my early work experience. The first lesson was that working hard wasn't the answer to earning more. The second lesson was that people often compromise their true potential because of what they have come to accept as their "lot in life." Their "internal computer programs" are so strong and so ingrained that they feel there is no hope of having more than what someone else tells them they're worth.

By seventeen, I had dropped out of high school. I got married at eighteen and started a family, with my first son being born when I was nineteen. My first real job was at a gas station, where I worked ten hours a day, six days a week, for one dollar per hour. My take home pay was $52.10 a week. It was a hard job and I worked hard. But for all my hard work, after a year I was still earning one dollar per hour. Again, it re-affirmed that working hard wasn't the answer to earning more.

My next job was working on an assembly line in a factory. I made $1.67 per hour, but I could only work forty hours a week, so I made about the same amount of money as at the gas station. I worked hard to perfect my efficiency, but even though I was one of the top workers in the factory, I was still paid the same. I was beginning to get it—you could only earn so much trading your time for money working with your own two hands.

After five years at the factory and going nowhere, I was introduced to direct selling in a business of my own. I was an "entrepreneur!" I couldn't spell the word, but I was one! I got the bug. The moment I was introduced to the concept, a light went on in my head, and right then I became "unemployable." I knew that I could never work for anyone again.

I went through a lot of ups and downs the first few years, especially the first year (more about that later). But I never lost that entrepreneurial spirit—the light never went out and it still burns brightly today.

SHARING MY SECRETS

I have been involved with many entrepreneurial ventures, from marketing various consumer goods to formulation of nutritional products, from owning medical clinics to home building, from infomercial marketing on television to publishing, and many others. Was every venture successful? No. But I learned just as much from the unsuccessful ones as from the successful ones.

As I gained more experience and became more successful in multiple businesses, I wanted to share my knowledge and my newfound freedom with others. I resolved to make a significant contribution toward helping men and women capitalize on their talents to achieve more satisfying lives. Because of my professional experience and success as an entrepreneur, I decided to begin coaching and training others on how to be successful.

Over the last three decades, what has captured my attention and the majority of my effort has been sharing what I learned about being a successful entrepreneur. Others who want more out of life—who want to enjoy greater financial achievement—have listened and learned, and I have heard many success stories where I played a part. I have had the opportunity to work as a consultant, a trainer, and a success coach to over three hundred companies and their employees. I have shared my entrepreneurial insights in seminars with more than a million people from all walks of life. I've utilized these principles to coach thousands toward greater success, and many of them have gone from being average wage earners to earning fortunes in their own business.

Whether you are already in a business of your own and want to take it to a new level, or you want to learn how to become a successful entrepreneur, I'll help you discover the missing piece to that elusive financial puzzle. I promise that when you learn to work freely and easily with the principles in this book, your business will become "intentionally successful."

1

Live the American Dream

Someday—what an interesting concept. Think of all the things that were supposed to have happened by now, that "someday" you convinced yourself was just around the corner. Think of all the energy you've expended wondering why that someday never seems to get any closer to becoming reality. Think of all the times you've wished you could live your life on your own terms, accomplishing your own goals instead of supporting someone else's. To most of us, that "someday" is where we've convinced ourselves we would be right now, if only we had more time, more talent, more money, or a better opportunity.

You may be looking for that perfect idea to start a business of your own. Or maybe you already have that perfect idea but just don't know where to begin. Maybe you have a great idea that just needs some refining. I don't know where you are today financially or in business, but I do know that, no matter where you are or what your circumstances, you have the talent hidden inside, waiting to be discovered, to take you toward achieving your most ambitious goals.

A SUCCESS STORY

Can an immigrant who doesn't know the marketplace or where to begin make it as an entrepreneur starting with nothing? "Yes," says Tony O'Donnell, owner of G.W. Health Products, based in Los

Angeles, California. Tony's beginnings were humble. Born the youngest of a family of eleven children in Donegal, Ireland, he spent his childhood doing all the typical boy things, playing sports such as soccer and making mischief. As the youngest of the family, he was a bit of a clown and prankster and did not apply himself to his studies.

Sixteen years ago, Tony emigrated from Ireland. He arrived in Los Angeles at the age of thirty-two with no immigration papers and only five hundred dollars to his name. But he also possessed a burning desire to show his family back in Ireland that he was not, as he puts it, "a bum," as well as a goal of making a difference in the lives of other people.

He tried various ways to make a living, including jobs in direct-selling companies. His goal of helping other people, he decided, would work best if he had his own business, and with that in mind he began selling herbal supplements and nutriceuticals directly to customers. His marketing consisted of handing out leaflets and brochures for his products in shopping centers and parking lots, anywhere he could reach large numbers of people.

In the beginning, Tony set only short-term goals: to feed himself and pay the rent for three months, then the next three months, and so on. To achieve that, he made it a daily routine to expose his health products to as many people as possible. He says he listened to motivational tapes every day, including mine, to stay on top mentally. And his faith helped him when he had doubts about his ability to succeed.

After seeing how much the natural products helped people, Tony became very excited about the value of the supplements he was selling. He developed a firm conviction that he could satisfy both his goal of helping people to make their lives better and of becoming successful in business.

His success led him to publish a book, *Miracle Super Foods That Heal,* and to co-author a book with the author of the best-selling *Vitamin Bible,* Earl Mindell. That book, *Greens are Good for You,* has been a runaway seller on Amazon.com. Today, Tony is a millionaire running a multimillion dollar business, with three television infomercials running. He credits much of his success to his faith and the education he received from the motivational tapes that were his constant companion. He says that aligning himself with, and learning from, the best people in the business has been a huge factor in his success.

THE CHOICE IS YOURS

So, the next time you overhear a friend or co-worker chattering enthusiastically about "SOHO," he or she is probably not talking about the fashionable SoHo district in New York City. In today's business world, *SOHO* refers to "small office/home office," like Tony's. It's one of the biggest explosions in the economy today, and a new frontier for millions of people. The small office/home office was born out of necessity. In an era when large corporations are only thinking of downsizing, many people are seeking a new way to sustain themselves financially.

In today's job world, the problem for many people is that most companies have no loyalty to their employees—their only loyalty is to the bottom line. And the bottom line is where many people find themselves when it's time for their employer to cut back. Our lives can be turned upside down because we have no control over our future. Unfortunately, our future gets discussed behind closed doors, probably by someone who has no clue about our loyalty to the company or our level of performance. They don't think about the fact that we have to pay bills, send our children to college, and pay the mortgage. This "decision maker's" job is to be impersonal and unbiased in all areas except the company's bottom line. In other words, to them, we really don't matter.

Maybe you are one of the few people who doesn't have to worry about such things, or maybe you've already achieved all you want to. If, however, you are like most people, the ones who have given up some of their desires and aspirations along the road of life, you do have a choice. So, the next time you rush out the door at 5:30 A.M. to get an early start and beat the traffic, or you get stuck on the freeway, or you miss your commuter train, and you find yourself worrying about whether you will have a job tomorrow, stop and think, "I do have a choice." Right now there are people just like you who are making a choice, taking control of their lives, and taking action toward a better future. They are taking advantage of the incredible free enterprise system and earning more money than they ever dreamed possible.

This ability to reach for your dreams is what the American dream is all about. And with today's technology, you can live where you want, work from home or in a small office, spend more time with the family, and control your own financial destiny. *You can have it all!* If you have a burning desire to change, you want to get ahead financially, you have an idea that needs some refining or you have a business that you want to start or take to the next level, you can start today to turn your ideas into goals, your goals into actions, and your actions into success!

We're living in the most affluent economy ever, and no sector of the economy is as essential, as creative, or as dynamic as small business. Small business is a world largely ignored by the mainstream press, yet for the past thirty years there has been an entrepreneurial explosion that has influenced every industry, every city and small town, and every ethnic group in this country. The explosive growth of small and home-based business continues to be an extremely important aspect of the economy.

The small business industry is building links among research, technology, state-of-the-art products, services, and consumer goods to meet society's demands. It is the beginning of a revolution. In my training programs, I've met doctors, carpenters, attorneys, writers, accountants, factory workers, teachers, and high school dropouts who are thriving in businesses they created from home. No matter what you do for a living, whether or not you are educated, whether or not you have business experience, if you find yourself thinking, "There must be a better way, a smoother road," well, there is!

The first key to finding a different road is a road map. If you just drive aimlessly through life feeling that you have one foot on the gas and the other on the brake, going nowhere fast, you'll continue to find yourself lost and tired. Eventually, you will give up on your goals and dreams. Even though many people in America—and throughout the world—are rich in talent, creativity, and resources, 95 percent of the population will give up on their dreams and end up broke. None of them ever thought it would happen to them. Wouldn't you rather map out your route to success and achieve all your goals and dreams? Wouldn't you rather be a success and have it all? Why not you? Don't you think it's your turn to succeed, to be one of the 5 percent who are financially free?

Whether your dreams are big or small, they can become a reality. The decision is yours, and the tools are all right there for you. It's time to take action, but will you?

FINDING THE AMERICAN DREAM

What does the American dream mean to you? Owning your own business, financial freedom, time freedom? Is the dream an illusion or a reality for you?

The classic version of the American dream is the story of the ant and the grasshopper. The ant works hard in the withering heat all summer long, building his house and laying up supplies for the winter. The grasshopper thinks the ant is a fool and laughs and dances and plays the summer away. Come winter, the ant is warm and well fed, while the grasshopper has no food or shelter and is left to suffer and die in the cold.

Here's the modern version of the American dream. The ant works hard in the withering heat all summer long, building his house and laying up supplies for the winter. The grasshopper thinks the ant is a fool and laughs and dances and plays the summer away. Come winter, the shivering grasshopper calls a press conference and demands to know why the ant should be allowed to be warm and well fed while he is cold and starving. The news media shows contrasting pictures of the shivering grasshopper and the ant in his comfortable home with a table of food. The world is absolutely stunned by the sharp contrast. How can it be that, in a country of such wealth, this grasshopper is allowed to suffer so? Is this fair? Shouldn't the ant share some of his food with the grasshopper? The case is made, and everyone is led to believe that the poor grasshopper is the victim, denied the prosperity he deserves by others who benefited unfairly.

Does this story sound like fiction or does it sound true to life? Consider the following statistics: 85 out of 100 people who reach the age of sixty-five do not have an extra hundred dollars; 45 percent are dependent on relatives for their survival; 30 percent depend on charity; 23 percent are still working; and only 2 percent are financially self-sustaining. According to the Social Security Administration, these numbers are the reality. In other words, at the age of sixty-five, chances are you'll still be working for someone else, making money for them, with your dreams unrealized. Most people will have no nest egg for retirement, their dreams deferred. I find this scenario frightening. I'm sure nobody thinks it could ever happen to them, but statistics say you will almost certainly end up there unless you take specific actions to avoid it.

Do people plan for failure to happen? No, they simply don't have a plan for it to *not* happen. How about you? Do you have all you want at this point in your life? Do you take the vacations you want every year or spend quality time with your family? Is your level of success or financial freedom today where you thought you would be ten years ago?

Here is the "old school" capitalistic version, which gives the story of the ant and the grasshopper a different slant. The grasshopper isn't really lying around doing nothing, he is becoming a better fiddler. And while his brain is at work devising new ideas, he makes friends with a butterfly who teaches him to fly. So, when winter comes, he has perfected the art of flying, and he flies south. He is now basking in the sun and making beautiful music while the ant is shivering in his bed, under the snow, as he eats his crumbs.

Here's the modern entrepreneurial or "enlightened capitalism" version. While the ant is busy gathering food for the winter, the grasshopper does his part by providing the music and song, because the world needs both ants and grasshoppers to survive. It takes both the serious and the artistic mind to create balance. While the ants are busy studying reports or clicking away at their computers, the grasshoppers are dreaming their way through a new symphony yet to be composed, a book yet to be written, a new idea to help others live a more fulfilling life, or a new product needed in the marketplace. I rather like this version, don't you? Work together, learn from one another, help others get what they want and everyone wins!

Whatever version you may have chosen in the past, today requires re-inventing yourself to become a modern-day entrepreneur.

YOU ARE THE STRONGEST LINK

Stop right now and take a realistic look at the last ten years. Have you truly made progress? Were your last ten years all that you wanted them to be? What's your plan for the future, for the next ten years and beyond?

There are no guarantees in life, but what I'm going to suggest to you is something you may have already concluded: for things to change in your life, *you've* got to make them change. For things to change, you have to make two important decisions. First, make a serious decision about the structure and direction of your life. You need a vision of how you want your life to turn out. Second, decide what *vehicle* you will use to take you where you want to go.

You can wait for better breaks, lower taxes, pay raises, better timing, another chance, or more and better opportunities. Many people do. But where do you really think that will lead? Again, look at the statistics. Some people continue to believe that education, environment, government, and other outside circumstances control their financial future, so they go to school to get a better education in hopes that they might land a better job.

There are tremendous shifts taking place in this country today, shifts that make it essential for those with low, average, and even high incomes to look for new ways to supplement their earnings. People do not feel secure. Few people succeed with the age-old model of "go to school, get a job, and retire in thirty or forty years." It is estimated that the average college graduate will change careers seven or eight times during his or her lifetime. That doesn't mean that college is a bad thing—it simply means that, in most cases, formal education is not the one vehicle that will take you where you want to go financially.

Today, people are discovering that the only way out of the trap is by taking responsibility for their *own* future, instead of leaving it to someone else or to chance. And because of that discovery, millions of people have turned to, and are succeeding in, home-based or other small business as a means of securing their financial future. If you review the possibilities in the marketplace, for the average person, running his or her own business is the most viable method of achieving financial freedom. It is estimated that within the next decade, 75 percent of all consumer goods will be marketed through home-based or small business. That trend toward entrepreneurship is the ground floor of a new revolution. The timing couldn't be more perfect. If you have the desire and the willingness to put forth some effort, it is time to create an action plan.

I often get asked, "Isn't the failure rate really high in home-based and small businesses?" The reality is that it's no higher than in any other type of business. However, a failure statistic is not what you should be concerned about. Your concern has to center on how to become a success. This is one of the most important points I want to make. A person can choose an opportunity, start their own business or enter a joint venture with a good company, have the best product, the best management, the best profit structure, and the best marketing system, and still not make a dime.

Look around you—we all know great people who work with good companies, or who have their own business selling consumer products like computers, clothes, cars, or nutrition, yet they're not coming close to achieving financial freedom. You may even have already tried home business opportunities. There are lots of them out there: 900 numbers, network marketing programs with fantastic products, nutrition products, servicing bubble gum machines, billing services, and so on. You may have even had some success, but you are not yet where you want to be. In any business opportunity, you always find successes and failures.

Here's my point: regardless of the job, profession, opportunity, or business (whatever your situation might be), whether or not you're successful is *not* determined by external factors like the company, product or marketing system—your success is determined by *you*. All those other factors are very important, but the number one factor that will determine your success is you. In order for things to change in your life, *you* have to be willing to make a change. If you continue to do what you've always done, you'll continue to have what you've always had.

You can change jobs, change your hair color, change professions, change geographic locations, change opportunities, but nothing will produce any lasting result until you decide to change. Trying to handle a new problem with the same old thinking that created it in the first place will not work. If you want a different result, you must *do something in a different way*.

You've no doubt witnessed a fly beating its head against a window trying desperately to get to freedom. It's a life-or-death struggle, a futile attempt to get through the glass, but the fly is using up the last energies of its short life. If you listen to the sound of its wings hitting the window, you can tell that the fly must be thinking, "Try harder." But it's just not working. No matter how much frenzied effort he expends bumping the window, the fly still has no hope for freedom. The real problem is that the fly's struggle is part of the trap. It's absolutely impossible for the fly to try hard enough to actually succeed in breaking through the glass, but he is willing to stake his life on reaching his goal using effort and determination alone.

You and I both know that the fly is doomed to die, even though a few feet away is an open door. With just a few seconds of flying time in the right direction, it could be free from its self-imposed trap and with only a fraction of the effort. The possibility is certainly there and it would be so easy if the fly could just see it. You have to wonder why the fly doesn't take another approach. How did he get so locked into this particular course? He must be sure that determined effort offers the most promise of success. And he continues to beat his head against the glass until he dies. Without a doubt, this approach makes sense to the fly, otherwise he would stop!

The point is that trying harder is not the solution to achieving more. In fact, often it is part of the problem, not the solution. If you rely on trying harder to accomplish all your hopes and dreams, you will surely end up with more of the same, and more struggle. To get a different result, you must do something differently.

FOR CIRCUMSTANCES TO CHANGE, YOU HAVE TO CHANGE

How would you rate your performance in life up until now? Do you feel that you are expending a lot of effort for the results you're producing? Do you feel you have to struggle for what you achieve? Until now, you've probably simply used your intuition to measure your performance. Unfortunately, this "gut feel" measurement is too ill-defined to be of any real value, because there's no way to pinpoint which aspects of your performance need improvement. Or maybe you take a different approach—you compare yourself to someone else as a measure of your own success. This approach can be frustrating and will lead you nowhere. There will always be those who achieve less or more than you with less or more talent, education, experience, capitalization, and so on.

Think about this: It is impossible to know what you don't know, and it is impossible to make improvements, until you know what needs to change. For example, you may know that your attitude stinks, but you don't know exactly how to change it. You may realize that you have a long list of unfulfilled dreams and you hate your job, but do you know how that came to be or how to make the necessary changes to correct your circumstances? Is it lack of focus on priorities, lack of people skills, or an inability to make clear-cut plans that support your goals? When you can't identify specific aspects of your performance that need changing, nothing changes. So, to remedy this condition, we're going to take a new approach and illuminate your perspective toward success by viewing your performance in a different light, one that will show you exactly which aspects of yourself may need improving.

Years ago, I was interviewing a young man in a business I was building. I asked him what income he was expecting to earn in his first year and in his second. He said, "I plan to earn $100,000 my first year, and at least a 50 percent increase in my second year."

Next, I asked what was the highest income he had ever earned in a single year. His answer? "$20,000." I then asked him if he thought he was worth $100,000 a year and he hesitantly responded, "I don't know, I think so."

My last, and most important, question was, "What do you plan to change about yourself to go from being a $20,000-a-year person to being a $100,000-a-year person?" And his answer was, "I don't know."

Here's my point: if a person considers him or herself to be a $20,000-a year person, he or she will never become a $100,000-a-year person without making some sort of change. There is *always* something that we need to change in order to further our progress and move to the next level of success. Here are some examples:

- Maybe it's simply having a new opportunity available and getting inspired by that opportunity.

- Maybe it's a matter of focusing and being fully committed to something for a longer period of time.

- Maybe it's learning and applying some new concepts.

- Maybe it's refining your people skills.

- Maybe it's gaining self-confidence.

- Maybe it's developing the courage to take a risk.

• Maybe it's changing one or more of your self-limiting beliefs or bad habits.

• Maybe it's simply a matter of "letting go" of some immobilizing fear.

• Maybe it's being willing to step out of your comfort zone.

• Maybe it's developing a new "mind-set."

I'll be expanding on many of the above items in the pages ahead. Increasing your personal effectiveness with giant strides, going from the "you" that you are now to the "you" that you want to become, will not come through applying conventional methods. Unconventional success in any endeavor will require unconventional approaches. It will require changing your behavior, your habits, and your thinking. It will require using "uncommon sense." In other words, you must take actions that may contradict "common sense."

The problem is that average people most often go with the obvious. We rely on the same thinking, habits, and behaviors we've used to get where we are now. We do this because we are attached to our old ways. Productive or not, our old ways are what we know. We are comfortable with them and we are not very willing to make a change. In fact, most of us are like the fly on the window, trying harder and harder, doing more of the same and getting nowhere fast. We resist new approaches because they make us feel more at risk, more uncomfortable.

But if you want rich rewards, rapidly, you must vigorously search out and implement new attitudes and behaviors. You must be willing to break free of old routines to find a better approach. What has worked for you in the past may have lost its viability. Even if your current approach is taking you in the direction you want, it may have to be changed periodically, maybe drastically at some point, in order to hit higher levels of achievement.

When we find our performance slackening a bit, we all have the tendency to rely on our old behaviors, but doing so creates a trap that ultimately leads nowhere. What I'm saying is that your most dependable behaviors can become your greatest obstacles for future success if you are not careful. They will become personal boundary lines that limit what you accomplish.

FALL "IN LOVE"

Achieving great things does not happen if you are not "in love" with what you want. Being in love involves being passionate, and passion is a very important part of the process. It lifts your spirit and energizes your heart and mind to move forward, faster, into a higher level of performance. Passion provides the fuel to keep moving forward when you hit obstacles or when you face uncertainty.

Your passion is fueled through your vision of what you want in your life. You must have an emotional intensity within you that burns hot enough to protect you when you meet setbacks, criticism, and other obstacles that interfere with your dream. And only deep passion for what you want can generate the heat needed to stay on target no matter what happens. Of course, for you to have such burning passion there must be something worth caring about, something inspiring enough to light the fire in your heart.

This means that you have to let go of the limits you have set on your thinking. Feed the feelings that fuel your passion and give yourself permission to go after what you want most. Give yourself permission to be successful. The time will be right for you to accomplish something great only when you are passionately drawn to it, so let your deepest desires direct you. Set your sights high enough so that you challenge yourself to live fully. Otherwise, a part of you remains asleep and your talents remain hidden.

Set your course. Make sure that you have a burning desire, a desire strong enough to move you past wishful thinking. Let your dream consume you and drive you to action. Remember, accomplishing your dream will come through an act of loving it, through your passion and how much you care about what you seek. Your emotions hold the power that will allow you to go the distance, so let your heart take charge of your move forward! Your world will respond differently when you actually decide clearly what you want and then take decisive action. Your "someday" dreams will become real only when you decide to have them and that nothing else will do.

Think about this for a moment: The things you've accomplished in the past are those you decided to accomplish and you took decisive action to achieve them, isn't that true? Everything you have achieved is what you have decided to go for. You can repeat affirmations all day long, and you can "think positively" until time stands still, but neither will produce results. They are both simply wishful thinking. What you need is *correct thinking* backed up by *correct action.* It's not what you *do* that matters, it's what you *get done!* You have to decide what you want, see it in your mind, and then you must take correct action. That's the only thing that will shorten the distance between where you are now and your desired outcome.

Many people confuse desire with deciding and taking action. Most have a deep desire for realizing their dreams, but when their desire fails to materialize, they conclude that the dream cannot be theirs. The problem is that longing for something is not enough. If a person does not achieve their dream, it doesn't mean achieving it is not possible—it means that desire alone will not, and cannot, deliver results. What if Thomas Edison had stopped at his second or third attempt at creating the light bulb? We might all still be living in the dark. What if Henry Ford had quit after his first attempt at creating the internal combustion engine? We might all still be riding horses. Taking action on what we've decided to accomplish makes all the difference. When we firmly decide what we want and then begin reaching for it, we drastically increase the odds of achieving it. And the more times we reach for it, the more we increase the odds.

DON'T WAIT FOR SOMEONE ELSE

I recently interviewed a successful entrepreneur and friend of mine, Don Hobbs, co-founder of Hobbs/Herder Advertising. His is a great story about decision-making and taking action.

Jim: Hobbs/Herder Advertising is a tremendous success story. How did it all start?

Don: When Greg Herder and I started Hobbs/Herder Advertising twenty years ago, the ideas that would shape our philosophy started like all good ideas, with excited talk and dreams of the future. That idea has grown into a thriving business with over 110 employees today. We began as a seminar company training realtors. We would book the preview meetings to sell tickets to our seminars, do the previews, sell the tickets, do the data entry, etc. The night before the event you would find us at Kinko's photocopying our class workbooks. We would then present the seminar and the next day we would be doing the follow-up with our graduates. Greg and I literally worked every aspect of the business.

Jim: When did you realize that your idea was going to turn into a thriving business enterprise?

Don: Trying to find a more defined niche in the market, we discovered what got the most attention was the personal marketing brochure. Following an event, one of the realtors asked, "Who creates and prints the personal marketing brochures?" And Greg said without hesitation, "We do!" In my mind, I said, "We do?" That was the first I'd heard of it, but I decided to not question it and go with it. That led to the development of a more defined niche of personal marketing that we still focus on twenty years later.

Jim: You often hear horror stories about partnerships in business. Tell me why yours has been so successful.

Don: For many of the same reasons we have a great friendship, Greg and I have a successful business partnership. Our complementary personalities are different in type and we have different core skills. Greg's the strategist and operations person, while I am more of a "people person" and more active in the field. Now, we have a deepening management team, but in the early days, the combination of both our talents led to a cohesive and successful partnership. Together, we have the ability to look at each project from two completely different angles. We also respect each other's talents and know what the other person brings to the party.

Jim: I know having a great team is critical to the success of every business. What other team members played a role in your growth?

Don: About two years into the business, we were experiencing rapid growth and we needed someone with a whole new set of talents. We added our third partner, Janet Herder, who is very different from either of us. She had big business experience, having run a multimillion dollar company. Janet was great with employees, hiring, and building culture. She added an element of caring and turned our company into the family environment that we enjoy today. And we have a president, John Surge, and a developing management team who are taking us into our next twenty years.

Jim: How about decision making? Who's in charge of making those critical decisions?

Don: Our common vision for the business did not come from one giving in and the other feeling the victor, but from a foundation on good communication. Even the best of friends don't always communicate as they should, especially in business. As Janet has since retired, Greg, John, and I have meetings weekly or even more frequently, and are lucky to be able to come to an agreement on the dozens of daily decisions, from critical to casual.

Jim: As owners, do you and Greg view the future direction of your business in the same way?

Don: We obviously share a common goal for our business, and the key is that we always have. We decided long ago to focus on training and marketing for real estate agents and companies, drawing on our own experience and backgrounds. This specialization—serving a certain segment of the marketplace and serving them well—has been the cornerstone to our success.

Jim: What is the main focus of Hobbs/Herder Advertising?

Don: Early in our business development, we decided that scatter-gunning and trying to be all things to all people would not work. We decided that there was a niche market with realtors. Real estate agents are small, independent businesses within the broker's business. Even the ones who are with large, well-known companies like Century 21, Prudential, Coldwell Banker, or RE/MAX have to figure out how to build their own names and, frankly, how to separate themselves from other agents in their own company. There was then and, to a very large extent, there still is a huge void in the marketing available to realtors and the knowledge of how to do marketing well. Our market was born! We work with real estate agents on their marketing, creating professional personalized advertising material for individuals and companies. We help them to brand themselves using their own unique story.

A big part of our seminars and training for realtors is to get our clients to see that how they market themselves should be no different from how they see products marketed every day. Instead of searching out each individual sale, introduce yourself to a target market and keep yourself in their view. Stop looking for the next sale. Stop living deal-to-deal. The goal is to get their clients to know them and to call them when they are ready to buy or sell real estate. The aim for our own business was the same. And then, once customers came to us, they were customers for life. We train agents in all aspects of their own marketing, including print, email, website development, pamphlets, brochures, and so on.

Jim: You've made a great name for yourself in this particular market. What are some of your thoughts for a new entrepreneur starting their own business?

Don: There are several things I would share with an aspiring entrepreneur. One—don't wait for the other guy to help you get started. If I were to offer a single bit of advice to anyone who was about to start his or her own business, that would be it. Don't wait for someone else to help you and don't go at your business halfheartedly. Develop your own client list and find your own niche. Be original. Would you rather be part of the large pack selling computers or would you rather be selling your own unique website design program?

Two—many people realize they are good at doing something: selling, mechanics, sewing, or what have you. They have an entrepreneurial seizure and decide to start their own business. The problem is that they have no customers. Developing your customer base is not part of your business, it *is* your business. It's not just about what you are good at. If you have no customers, you have nothing. You may be the best buggy-whip maker in the world, but your business will not be successful if you don't locate customers to buy your product.

Three—go for a niche market, then brand yourself, your product, your storefront, your company, or whatever. By branding, I mean to make you or your product known in a personal and unique way to anyone who may be a prospective customer. Step out of the pack and make sure they know who you are and what you offer. Lots of places make hamburgers, but everyone knows what you are talking about when you say "Big Mac."

Four—ask for help. Do not be intimidated about calling someone who may be of assistance to you. A personal call, done politely, and going quickly to the point, lowers resistance.

Five—do not expect your business to be instantly successful. Financial return may be slow in coming initially. We live in an instant gratification society, but starting a business doesn't usually work that way. You have to invest first and, if you do it well, you may be here in twenty years to tell your story. You have to constantly monitor how your marketing is working. As you grow your business, your strategic plan may need anything from some fine-tuning to a complete change of direction. In today's marketplace, you have to re-invent yourself on a regular basis.

The most satisfying business for most people is one in which they help others with their lives. Being financially successful and having a high degree of personal satisfaction is as good as it gets. My first job after completing high school was selling seminars with you, Jim. That was nearly thirty years ago, and we still maintain contact. You never know when an old friend may be helpful to you or you may be helpful to them. My last gem of wisdom seems obvious, but in the "busyness" of business it is easy to forget: constantly widen your circle of acquaintances and friends. They will make your business easier and your life worthwhile.

YOU CAN'T WIN HALFWAY

Another great success story is about John, a man I met in Dallas a few years ago. In 1983, he was a broke college student. He was about to graduate, so he was weighing the job market. "To say the least, I was shocked by the lack of opportunity," he said. John went on numerous interviews for a co-editor position with small town sports-related newspapers. As exciting as a career in sports journalism may have sounded, these interviews offered him a chance to earn a whopping salary of around $12,000 a year. Not growing up in a wealthy family, John had financed his college education with a $40,000 student loan, so this yearly income just wasn't going to cut it.

Just prior to graduation, he was introduced to direct sales and network marketing by a friend and started to explore the possibilities. He discovered that some average people with average backgrounds were earning in many cases extraordinary incomes—that definitely got his attention. A short time later, he joined the business and attended a training seminar, where he heard the famous statement, "For things to change for you, you have to make a change. And for things to get better, you have to get better." He realized that he could be successful in this business with the correct knowledge. He started to get serious about learning from others who had already done well. John buckled down, worked hard, learned from his mistakes, learned from others already doing well, and developed the skills. In his first full year, John earned in excess of $30,000.

But it gets better! By 1989, just six years into the business, John had earned several million dollars. He was traveling the world and leading a lifestyle that most people only dreamed about. His business had grown into several countries, including Australia, Canada, and parts of Europe. Over twenty-five years later, he had more than $10 million in earnings and his business continued growing rapidly.

I asked John, "What has it been like to start with nothing, $40,000 in debt, and turn it into a thriving business that earns you a million dollars a year whether you work or not?"

"It feels great! As I look back, I have spoken before tens of thousands of people in forty-two countries, people just like myself who wanted a chance to do well financially. I feel like I have helped hundreds of people achieve their financial and entrepreneurial dreams and thousands more to put enough money in the bank to purchase a new home, send their kids through college, or help them to live a better lifestyle."

Then, I asked John what were the greatest lessons he learned that he could share with others walking the same or a similar path.

"First," he said, "Make a firm decision to do it, one that doesn't allow for retreat. Secondly, find a company and a product that you can believe in. Third, take action daily. Execute—get off your butt and work! And remember that a day that you don't take action toward building your business enterprise is a day that you are out of business. If you want to have a successful business, you have to commit yourself and have discipline to do whatever it takes. And last, and most important, don't be afraid to fail. I have discovered that the fear of failing is the exact thing that causes most people to fail. When my well-meaning friends and relatives told me that I was crazy and that this type of business wouldn't work, I had that small voice inside, along with a level of commitment that encouraged me to move forward. My message is simple. You can win but you can't win halfway."

GET ON WITH IT!

So, don't be afraid to fail. Get on with it—you can do it! If you knew me, you'd probably think you were smarter than me, and you probably are. You may think that you are harder working, and you may be. Then you might say, "How come you were so successful and some others weren't?" Here's why: I took advantage of every opportunity to grow my business. I saw every situation as either a chance to win or a chance to learn. I didn't always win but I did always learn, because I discovered early in my business career that if you don't learn, then you don't grow personally or financially. I was never afraid to fail, because I thought that even if the worst thing happened, I could always go back and take the $12,000-a-year job.

Winning at the game of wealth is based on the premise of deciding and taking action. Winning requires that you take the offensive. You can't achieve great things in a defensive posture or from a passive position. You've got to make a move on your dream and that means stepping out of your safety net of "faint hope" and taking decisive action now. I don't know what may be holding you back, but you do. If you just stop for a moment and observe yourself (you will have ample opportunity to do so as you progress through this book), you can look for outdated behaviors and beliefs that keep you where you are now. The bottom line is this: For things to change in your life, you have to change. Nothing changes until you do!

2

Be Your Best at Whatever You Do

Everything you need to be successful as an entrepreneur you already possess. You have the opportunity and the power to perform—those traits are inside *you,* not in the situation you may be experiencing. You already have the answers, whether you know it or not. For any questions that remain, the answers must come from within. What I will be doing is simply pointing the way. All you have to do is "tune in" and listen to yourself, because no one else can hear those voices.

Your dreams and desires that burn the hottest create the magnetic energy that points the way to your objective. When you look inside and discover what pulls at your consciousness, you'll find your way unfolding before you. So, put your best foot forward and trust that you are moving in the right direction. If you're not, you'll feel it in your gut and you can take immediate action to change.

THE "ENTREPRENEUR LIGHT"

I'd like to share a couple of meaningful business experiences that happened to me over the years. My first job was working in a gas station. I never had a goal of being in my own business or any other plan for my life, at least not consciously. I always had those "someday" dreams just like everyone else, but that was about it. After all, as a high school dropout, what chance did I have of getting ahead in life? I worked sixty hours a week with no overtime pay. My wage was one dollar per hour and my take home pay was $52.10 a week. I liked my job and I always strove to do the best job I could. In fact, I believed that I was the best gas station attendant in the whole world.

When customers would come in, I would give them the very best service they had ever experienced. I would greet them with a smile and ask them how I could be of service to them.

I would check their oil, check the air in their tires, wash their windshield, sweep out their car, and then ask them what else I could do for them. And when I would bring back their change, I would enthusiastically thank them and tell them how much we appreciated their business, and to please come again.

There was a man who worked with me (we'll call him John). John was a habitual complainer. When a customer would come in, he would complain, "It's too hot," or "It's too cold," or "Don't they know that it's closing time?" He complained about everything. When John would go out to greet a customer, he would never say, "May I help you?" He would simply walk up to the car and say, "Yip!" What did that mean? He would never check the tires or wash the windshield unless he was asked to do so, and only then with a pained look on his face. And when he would take back their change, he would just plop it in their hand and walk away.

One day, I went through my whole service routine with a customer and brought him back his change. As I walked away, he got out of the car, and said, "Excuse me, young man, but could I ask you a question? What are you doing working in this gas station?" I said, "Well, it's my job." And he said, "And you are very good at it too. You're the only one here I want to wait on me. In fact, I won't let that guy wait on me." He pointed toward John. "The reality is, I live on the other side of town and there are gas stations over there, but I like having you take care of me. I even know your days off and I don't buy gas on those days."

I had no idea anyone felt that good about my service except for me. He went on to say, "You have a lot more on the ball than working in this station. You ought to be working in the factory on the assembly line." I said, "I could never qualify for that job because I don't have a high school diploma." He explained that he was one of the supervisors and that he could arrange for me to be hired if I could pass a simple test.

I passed the test and got the job. Two weeks later, I was working in the factory, making $1.67 an hour. What I didn't realize was that I only got to work forty hours each week instead of my usual sixty at the gas station, so I still took home about $52 each week. At least it was shorter hours for the same pay.

The thing I noticed at the factory almost immediately was that almost everyone I worked with complained about their jobs, just like John did. The only difference was that there were several thousand of them. They complained about their hours, their shift, and their co-workers. They complained if they had to work overtime and they complained if they didn't get to work overtime.

My job was wiring a certain type of circuitry. I was allotted a specific amount of time to complete each part of the job, then I was rated on my efficiency. With 85 percent efficiency or over, they couldn't fire you; at 100 percent you got placed into a bonus pool where you received a small monthly bonus based on the whole group's efficiency. No matter how good any individual might be, there was very little bonus earned because of poor performers, but it was better than nothing and I accepted it graciously.

After about a year or so of working at the factory, I was doing the job of several people. I could produce more in less time than anyone. I never had a thought or goal of something better. I was a factory worker, I liked my job, and I took pride in being good at it. One day, a man from the next department approached me and asked, "Hey, Britt, are you going to work in this factory the rest of your life?"

I said, "I don't know, maybe." And I didn't know.

He said, "Why don't you come to a meeting with me tomorrow night? I think it might be something you and I could do part time and earn some extra money."

That's how I ended up in my first business! At the end of my first year in that business, I was failing miserably. I was not a failure, but I was failing. A failure gives up, and that was one thing I wasn't willing to do. I'll tell you more about my first business later. The one thing I can tell you is that the "entrepreneur light" came on in my head that first night at the meeting, and it wouldn't go out. I decided that night to become responsible for my own future, to never again allow anyone to tell me how to live my life and how much money I could earn. And because I refused to give up, within six months from the end of my first year of earning virtually nothing, I was well on my way to becoming a millionaire.

A few years later I was offered an opportunity to join someone in the business of promoting seminars to the general public. We were the first company I know of to do that. I had assembled a team that sold tickets to events by the tens of thousands and I had become, in a short period of time, the best seminar promoter in the world.

FACE YOUR FEARS

I was asked one day to make a presentation to a group of about fifty people. I said "yes" without even thinking about it. There was a big problem, though—speaking was my greatest fear. After I said "yes," I was literally panic-stricken. It was booked for a couple of months in the future and I was sick for nearly two months. You could probably better describe it as "terrified."

Finally, the day arrived. I spent the entire night before trying to come up with a good excuse to get out of doing the presentation. I had to leave for the speech at about 8 A.M. At about 7:30, I came up with the answer to get out of it—I decided that I was going to have an accident in my car on the way. Not a bad one, but one that would give me a legitimate excuse for not showing up.

Just as I reached for the hotel door to leave, there was a knock. Thinking it was the maid, I opened the door and there stood the man who had scheduled me for the talk.

He said, "I've come to pick you up."

My first thought was, "You are going to be in the accident too!" I said, "I'll drive."

He said, "No, I'll drive." We went back and forth several times and finally he said, "I'm parked in front of the door, so I'll drive. I know the way." My excuse was blown!

At the event, I was so nervous that I don't remember much about it. I spoke for about twenty minutes and have no idea what I said. All I can remember is that when I finished, there was applause. I didn't know if they were clapping because it was over or because they liked it. Either way, I didn't really care because I just wanted out of there.

I immediately went to my friend's car and sat inside to regroup. I thought to myself, "Never again will I feel that way." I realized I had two choices. One was to never do it again, which was certainly what I was considering. The other was to do it often and get good at it. I thought about it for a few more minutes and realized that I didn't have it in me to give up, so I chose option number two.

I was in charge of a large sales staff that promoted the seminars for us. Back at the office, I told the whole group at our next sales meeting that I would present any talk for them with over fifty people in attendance. And I did, sometimes several a day, for the next five years. That's one way to overcome your fear—massive action. Over the years, I have lectured before more than a million people and to audiences as large as 10,000. Now I haven't heard all the speakers in the world, but last year I did receive the "Speaker and Trainer of the Year" award in one of the direct sales associations. I may or may not be the best, but in my mind I am as good as anyone.

People kept telling me that I should write a book about my life. I had made one attempt to write one—more of a "how to" book on personal growth—but it didn't go well, and I never thought I could do it. I thought, "Who would want to read about me and my experiences?" Plus, my worst subject in school was English: I failed it with flying colors—straight F's. But after a lot of encouragement from those attending my seminars, even though I had no idea how to begin, I made the decision to write a book. I did hire someone to help me with that first book, but it did get written.

My first book was called *Rings of Truth.* Guess what? It's the best book that's ever been written—at least it is in my mind. In fact, the publisher called me after he had read the manuscript and told me that most of his staff concurred that it was one of the best books they had ever read. Later, I received a call from a publisher in Norway who had been publishing self-help books for over twenty years. He said, "Having published hundreds of books in this field, I've had the opportunity to read thousands of self-help books. In my opinion, *Rings of Truth* is the best book that has ever been written and the most important book except for the Bible." Darn, I guess I missed it by one!

This is my sixth book and guess what? It's the best book that's ever been written. In fact, all of my books are the best books that have ever been written. And my next one will also be the best book that's ever been written.

Now, I've told you this series of stories for a reason. It's not to brag about being the best gas station attendant, soap salesman, seminar leader, or author, even though I was. Here's my point: *Be the best that you can be at whatever it is you do.* Why not? If you are going to do it anyway, why not do it the best you can? You don't have to be "the best"—what I'm saying is to be "your best."

DO YOUR BEST

If you are going to build a business, give it your best shot. Don't do it halfheartedly! If you are going to make a presentation to a prospect, give it everything you've got. Put the best you have into everything you do. Here's another way of saying it: When you do what you do with love, you'll eventually have only what you love in your life. Fall in love with what you do, whatever it may be, and give it your best shot.

I never planned to be the best gas station attendant or the best factory worker or the best soap salesman. I never planned to be in the speaking field and receive an award for being the best in an industry. I never planned to become a writer. But I always planned to do my very best.

Here's what I believe happens when you give your best. Because I gave it my best at the gas station, someone invited me to work at the factory. Someone was looking over me and said, "Well, he's become the best and that was his goal. I suppose we should present him with another opportunity for growth and to be his best. Let's make a factory worker out of him and see how he does." Because I gave it my best at the factory, someone invited me to a meeting. Someone was looking over me and said, "Well, he mastered this one too, let's make a soap salesman out of him and see how he does at that."

Because I gave it my best as a soap salesman, someone invited me to join a seminar company. "Speaking is his greatest fear, let's see how he does at this one." Because I was presenting seminars, I gained the knowledge, along with my past experiences, to write books. Someone said, "Let's make a writer out of him. English was his worst subject and he thinks he can't write. Let's challenge him with this one and see how he does."

Here's my point: When you are being your best at whatever it is you do, it leaves you open for great opportunities to come your way. If you are in the dumps, if you have a bad attitude, if you complain all the time, if you hate your current circumstances, if you live in anxiety about the past or the future, then you are not open to receiving new opportunities. You probably would not even recognize opportunities when they were presented, because who would want to offer that sort of person an opportunity to invest in their business, or even buy from them?

To whom would you respond favorably—the person being his or her best or to the complainer? Opportunities aren't available for people who don't strive to be their best at whatever they do. Complainers won't recognize opportunities because they're too busy complaining for anything new to enter their lives. They are too busy being victims, complaining about what's wrong, to be successful. When you strive to be your best, people, opportunities, and the right circumstances will flock to you like flies to honey.

If you are going to build a business, why not build the best one that's ever been built? If you are going to give a meeting for your company, why not give the best meeting that's ever been given? Victims complain about their circumstances and how few opportunities there are, but winners do something about it. Victims complain about how others are not doing it right and are hurting their business, while winners just get the job done by focusing on success and taking action to achieve it. When winners are faced with an obstacle, they don't complain, they simply take a step to the left and move past it.

You may not be *the* best, but that doesn't matter. All I'm saying is make it *your* best. Why not? You'll be pleasantly surprised at the results you produce when you put your best foot forward. You'll be surprised at how it makes you feel, and feelings are what attract circumstances into your life and into your business. When you feel good, good things happen.

Fall in love with being your best. *When you do what you do with love, you will eventually have only what you love in your life.* That's a powerful statement for any area of your life. Think about it as it relates to the law of cause and effect. When you are in love with your business, being your best, being financially free, being happy and fulfilled, having a better relationship, then you are putting the wheels in motion to attract the same thing back into your life many times over. When you look at it in that way, does it not make sense to be the best you can be at whatever you do? Even if you don't like your job, doesn't it make more sense to be your best so that you'll be open for better opportunities when they come along? In fact, being your best at whatever you do is absolutely critical to finding new opportunities in your life.

WHAT YOU BECOME, YOU ATTRACT

The person you become determines what you are handed next. *"If you do what you do with love, you'll eventually have only what you love in your life."* That doesn't mean that you necessarily have to love what you do, but treat it like you love it so that you give it your best.

The question I get asked most frequently is, "How do I know

what my purpose is in life? How do I know if I'm on the right track?" That's a complex question, but here's my simple answer: Whatever you are doing right now is what you are supposed to be doing. If you are working at a job you hate, until you start being the best you can at whatever it is you are doing, nothing will change. Circumstances won't change until you do. You can change jobs or move to a new city, but soon you'll be right back in the same position, attracting the same circumstances. Nothing changes until you actually make a change in you.

When we become the best that we can be at whatever we currently do, the door opens for circumstances to change. Circumstance then provides us with a new opportunity to become even better. I never even had a thought of leaving the gas station job, but as soon as I had become the best gas station attendant in the world (at least in my opinion), the universe went to work for me to provide a new challenge, a new opportunity, and a new level of growth to attain.

If you haven't learned all you can where you are currently, you don't get to move on to bigger and better things. That's the reason some people feel stuck, while others seem to be always moving on to better opportunities. The "stuck" people haven't learned all they need to in order to move to the next level; they haven't stepped up and stepped out of their comfort zone.

Do you want things to get better for you? Get on with it! If you observe your thoughts and behaviors drifting away from being the best you can be, simply return to the present and put forth your best effort. This should apply whether you're mowing the lawn, building your business, conducting a meeting, having a conversation with a friend, or eating dinner with the family. If you observe yourself drifting away in any way, *return to the present.* In other words, if you are at work, you should be working. If you are playing, you should play. If you are spending time with the family, you should be there with the family. If you are exercising, you should focus on what you are doing. Wherever you are, be there. And wherever that is, play full out and be your best!

THE RIGHT ATTITUDE

What exactly is attitude? When we think of attitude, we think in terms of a positive or a negative one. Attitude is a mental position or feeling with regard to something else. In other words, your attitude determines how you see the world around you. Saying it another way, what you see is who you are, and who you are determines what you see and what you receive as well.

Maintaining the right attitude will be an essential part of your self-management and your success. Attitude is not something that you "turn on" when you face a prospect or come to the office and then "turn off" when you leave. Your attitude is a reflection of who you are and what you honor in your life. Simply put, your attitude is a mind-set.

Some believe that their education, their environment, the amount of money they now have, and other outside circumstances control their success or failure. That is simply not true. It's not what happens to you that determines the quality or degree of your success, it is what you do about what happens that makes all the difference. It's what you honor that determines your success. It's your attitude or mind-set toward success that makes success happen, or not. We all have stuff to deal with—it rains on the rich as well as the poor. The very same circumstances can happen to different people, and yet some come out on top while others come to a stop, believing themselves to be a victim of circumstance or some cruel fate.

Your attitude is the starting point, the mechanism that turns on or shuts off the flow of ideas that can bring forth your success. With the right attitude, you'll become a powerful magnet for attracting pleasant experiences and the things you want in your life and your business. Your attitude toward your customers will determine their attitude toward you and your products. Your attitude toward life will determine how life treats you. Your attitude toward your business will determine how the business provides for you financially. It is vitally important to develop the right attitude, an attitude of aspiring. You should aspire to the following.

- Aspire to do well in your business.
- Aspire to give good service.
- Aspire to follow up.
- Aspire to help others on your team become successful.
- Aspire to have people respect your leadership abilities.
- Aspire to be non-judgmental toward yourself and others.
- Aspire to communicate well and have others listen to you.
- Aspire to listen to others with sincere interest.
- Aspire to present yourself well.
- Aspire to become a leader of leaders.
- Aspire to have people love your products or service.
- Aspire to "earn" the success you want and deserve.

There's a huge difference between "expecting" these things to happen and "aspiring" to have them happen. Expectation will most often end in disappointment. When you expect something to happen in a certain way or by a certain time and it doesn't, you become disappointed. For example, you can expect that all your prospects will buy, but what if they don't? You will be disappointed. On the other hand, you can aspire to have all your prospects become customers, and if some don't, you won't be disappointed because you did your best.

Aspiring to do something leaves you room to be flexible. If you aspire to reach the stars and only hit the moon, it's still okay. You are not disappointed because you gave it your best. You can aspire to do your best and allow others on your team to be their best in your presence. But when you expect to be *the* best, you compete with everyone on your team.

I've found that more often than not we get exactly what we truly aspire to have in our lives. The reason is that aspiration begins with what you honor in your life, the value you aspire to live by, not what you fear. Expectation is fear based, while aspiration is value based. Also realize that some people may not have the same values as you. You will often be disappointed if you expect everyone to value the same things. The result of your attitude will always show up on the bottom line, in the success of your business. It will show up in your bank account, in your overall happiness, in every area of your life.

Here are a few simple points that will help in maintaining the right attitude:

• *Continue to refine and develop your compelling "why."* Continue to refine the reasons you're involved in business, the reasons you want to be successful. This process helps you hold true to the real essence of why you are involved. Continue to refine the passion that drives your success.

• *Develop and implement a clear-cut strategy plan* for achieving your compelling "why." Remember, your team is watching you and will always follow your lead, either consciously or subconsciously. If you have a plan and follow it, your team will develop a plan that supports your plan and they will follow it. Even if you are a "shoot from the hip" entrepreneur and your plan is being refined as you go, it's still important to follow a plan.

• *Develop a strong "conviction"* about the value of your products and service. Your conviction will always come across in your presentation. If you are not sold, how could you expect someone else to be sold enough to buy?

• *Fall in love with what you're doing.* Remember your first love affair? That's how you should feel about your business.

• *Fall in love* with the potential of your opportunity.

• *Fall in love* with your team spirit.

• *Fall in love* with the value of your products.

• *Fall in love* with the challenge of being your best.

• *Fall in love* with being a good leader.

• *Fall in love* with being a leader of leaders.

• *Fall in love* with working on yourself, your own growth, and the value it brings into your life.

• *Fall in love* with the opportunity to make a difference in someone else's life.

• *Have a "do it now" attitude.* Develop a sense of urgency, not a sense of panic. You know exactly what you want to accomplish and you get the job done without hesitation.

• *Create a plan for your own development.* Your income will not far exceed your own personal growth. You will always receive exactly what you believe you are worth. If you don't grow personally to match your income growth, you may find that soon your income will shrink back to your size. Working on your own development and sense of self-worth will always pay you great dividends.

• *Become a risk taker.* Many people look only for the risk in the opportunity, and by doing so, they miss the opportunity altogether. Instead, develop the attitude of looking for the opportunity in the risk. For example, talking to strangers may feel risky to you. They might say "no." Instead, look for all the reasons they'll say "yes," ways that you can make it work, and focus your efforts on those things. Look for the opportunity that may be hidden within the risk. If you decide not to talk to a stranger because he or she might say "no" or might not want to talk with you, you have chosen to honor your fear instead of your success, to honor the risk instead of the opportunity the risk might bring.

• *Be innovative.* Always keep an open mind to new ideas and new possibilities. Look at it this way: What if you try something new and it doesn't work, what have you gained? You've gained experience, right? On the other hand, what if you don't try something new and it may have worked, what have you gained? Nothing. Be open to trying new things and new methods until you discover what works best for you.

Remember that your attitude is contagious, both to yourself and to others. Before you go to sleep at night, ask yourself these important self-management questions:

- What did my opportunity provide for me today?
- What did I do today to improve my business?
- Who did I talk to about my products today, and how did they respond?
- What could I have done differently today that might have worked better?
- What did I do today that really worked, and how could I implement that as a part of my daily routine?
- Who on my team needs my support tomorrow?
- Who on my team needs recognition and what can I do to recognize them?
- What did I do today to bring me closer to my goals and dreams?

SIX ATTITUDE TYPES

I find that there are basically six different types of attitudes that will determine your level of success.

The Poverty Attitude

People with this attitude can't fully commit to a given opportunity for any period of time. Fear runs their lives—they are afraid to move ahead because they might fail, or they jump from one opportunity to the next, sometimes even working three or four at the same time, faintly hoping that one of them will make them enough money to pay their bills this month. And that's about all they can expect. People with the poverty attitude will always place the blame on someone or something else for their lack of success. This attitude encourages a state of dependence.

The Paycheck-to-Paycheck Attitude

The paycheck-to-paycheck attitude is a step up from the poverty attitude. The person is always looking for job security and will take very few risks. He's the nine-to-fiver who wants his paycheck on Friday. The paycheck-to-paycheck attitude restricts personal initiative. The person with this attitude may even become bitter toward someone who is doing well or who breaks out of his or her own limiting attitude.

The Middle Income Attitude

The middle income attitude has allowed this country to thrive with a maximum amount of growth and freedom. This is usually a healthy attitude, one that accepts reality as it is. People with the middle income attitude usually experience some degree of growth throughout their life. The only problem is that their attitude toward money does not always prepare them to take the risks necessary to move to new levels financially. People with this attitude often end up spending their money for some kind of "get rich quick" scheme that rarely makes any money. They typically have the capacity to open up new exciting opportunities for financial growth, but they need to be open to the necessary coaching.

The Game Player Attitude

The game player attitude is the middle income attitude that, through coaching, has risen to a higher level. People with the game player attitude take someone else's game and play it to the maximum. Instead of earning $50,000 a year, they may be earning $150,000 to $200,000 a year. Over time, they may also develop the skills to earn even higher incomes. They may take risks, but usually only within their area of expertise.

The Game Maker Attitude

The game makers can create their own game or they can play

someone else's for a piece of the action. They usually create a lot of wealth both for themselves and for others around them. They see themselves not just as company owners but as partners with everyone involved. They are as much concerned about the success of everyone around them as they are with their own. They will spend a lot of time and energy accomplishing their objectives. They never criticize or complain, instead they look for solutions. The person with the game maker's attitude has a lot of self-confidence and usually makes a lot of money.

The Millionaire Maker Attitude

The millionaire maker attitude is the one you want to develop. We all have the ability to do so no matter where we start financially or what experiences we have had in business. The millionaire maker attitude actually frees you from money concerns and allows you to experience life and run your business from a whole new perspective. People with this attitude put money in its place, allowing them to concentrate their efforts on their business and on living their life to the fullest. The pleasures, freedom, and success this attitude brings are unlimited.

VALUE YOURSELF

Anyone can develop the millionaire maker attitude no matter what his or her circumstances or financial condition. How do you develop this attitude? You begin by looking at the wealth around you. What would you think of someone who had millions and complained of being broke? You'd probably have very little sympathy for him or her. Yet, many people complain because they do not see the wealth around them. Money is everywhere, and you simply have to develop the attitude necessary to recognize that fact in order to receive your share. Of course, when you really look at it, everybody is already receiving their share, what they think they deserve. To receive more, you have to change your attitude toward money and what you believe to be your share.

The first step is learning to use your imagination. Take all those old thoughts, feelings, and beliefs that you've developed about money over the years and if they're not working for you, toss them out! Get rid of them! You no longer need them. You can't go to the next level financially if you don't change the rules of the game you're playing. The thinking, beliefs, and attitude that got you where you are today will not take you where you want to go. If you want things to change in your life, you have to change, because circumstances won't change until you do.

It's also important to remember that your attitude toward money can be totally different from the reality of how things actually are in your life at the moment. In other words, you may not have money. That's a reality, not an attitude. The realities in your life may result from many outside circumstances: For example, you don't have enough money to start a business or you don't know how to go about raising capital to start a business. These are realities, and to change them may require learning certain new skill sets. Your attitude, on the other hand, reflects ways in which you evaluate and act upon what is happening, how you look at your circumstances or lack of experience. Again, it's not what happens to you that matters, it's what you do about what happens that counts.

Two partners go bankrupt in their business. One partner jumps out the window of a ten-story building. The other goes on a month-long vacation to regroup. When he comes back, he starts a new business and becomes very successful. True story. They both express an attitude, and each has a solution. One escapes by killing himself, while the other escapes to reclaim his attitude and begin again.

To develop the millionaire maker attitude, you need to see yourself as already having millions. Imagine for a moment that you had all the money you ever wanted. How would you act? How would you spend your day? How would you feel? What would you do with your time? What would you be doing with your life? Most people get stuck in the attitude, "As soon as I make some money, then I'll start living my life. Then I'll have a better attitude toward money." We constantly deny ourselves the opportunities and pleasures that are right in front of us because of our attitude and how we perceive the world. We can't see the opportunities and abundance around us because of our perceptions—we are focused on the problem instead of being open to finding a solution. Your perception is your reality. What is your perception? As a friend of mine, Jim Rohn, used to say, "Do you look through the window and see the beautiful sunset or do you see the specks on the window?"

Begin to think and act as if you already have money, as if money is no longer a problem in your life. Act as if you have the power and freedom that comes with having money, as if you have the ability to change your circumstances. If you made a million dollars a year in your business, how would you come across to a potential buyer if you were to sell your business? Would you be different? Would you have more confidence? Would you have a different viewpoint about money? If so, adopt that viewpoint and see what it does for your effectiveness and for your overall success now.

You don't have to have money to project an attitude of success. This is not lying to yourself, it's simply making the decision that nothing short of financial success will do. Your attitude now may be that you have no room for failure, or is it an attitude of lack? You will always attract to your life what you feel about yourself. The amount of money you attract into your life will be based upon the attitude you have about money, on how much you've decided you are worth. If you want to make a lot of money, if you want to attract a team of great partners to your business, start acting like having money is your natural state. Start acting like the leader that others would want to follow. You can't be poverty minded and attract money. You can't be a victim and attract winners—only winners attract winners!

What often happens is that people value what they don't have more than what they do have. A person without money would value himself more if he had money. Every time you catch yourself feeling envy toward someone else or feeling depression because you don't have certain things, you actually move your center of power *away* from your own strength. You focus on lack and that focus will result in weakness and insecurity. Before you can ever have millions, your attitude will have to be one of valuing where you are right now and moving toward where you want to be.

The number one secret to developing a millionaire maker attitude is to value yourself, to value your self-worth. Place no one else above you. Value and enjoy your own life because you continually put forth your best. When you value yourself, your value to others increases. When you come in contact with other people, you carry a presence that is powerful and effective. By developing and projecting the attitude of self-worth, you eliminate your struggles immediately. You can reach wealth that makes you feel content and secure, and you can begin right now by actually feeling content and secure.

A WEALTHY ATTITUDE

The quality of your life should never depend on how much money you have. With the right attitude, you'll discover that good health, great relationships, family fun, and most of the pleasure you find in life all operate outside the world of money. You become wealthy by learning to seek out and enjoy the things you want in life. It's called having a "wealthy" attitude. You can move this attitude into a state of being a millionaire; that's how millionaires become millionaires! They become one in their mind before they actually achieve it. Personal development, continually aspiring to do your best, leads you to the person you become inside and that attracts wealth into your life.

3

Make a Decision to Be Wealthy

This may come as a shock to you, but most people really don't want to change. Just give them a beer, point them toward the sofa, and give them the television remote. They will continue to complacently live out their lives. Most people are much too busy earning a living to become financially free. They spend the majority of their time focused on what they *don't have* and what they *don't want,* instead of focusing on what they *do want* in their lives. They let their current circumstances run their lives. They let their current job or earnings dictate what they can and can't do.

Most people operate with a mind-set that assumes success comes one step at a time. The unspoken assumption is that we must move systematically from our present level of achievement to the next. Once that level is reached, work begins toward the next incremental level, and so on. In other words, you must follow a gradual step-by-step process.

I don't believe this to be true at all, but it is clearly reflected in the way most people function. They go about their business day-to-day, trying hard to make some incremental improvements in their performance. That's the conventional way to grow, but life and business simply do not have to operate that way. At least not today. Although the typical conventional growth from where you are now to the next level up feels easier and more comfortable, even natural and safer, there's a much faster way. Instead of accepting the "norm" or being content with gradual improvement, why not take decisive action? Go for the gold!

THE CHOICE IS YOURS

If you want to become successful, if you want to become financially free, you have to take action to change, otherwise there will always be somebody telling you how to run your life, making you feel insecure and doubtful. I know people, as I'm sure you do, who go to work every day to a job that they hate. They hate what they earn and/or what they do, but they stay because they feel they have no other choice. They justify their position by calling it job security, but what they don't realize is that there's no security in a job. It's called "prolonged poverty" in my book!

It's like living in a place you hate, but you're afraid to move because of your job. Then you lose your job and can't afford to move, so you look for another insecure position that will keep you in the place you hate. That sounds like insanity, don't you think? Someone asked me one day what I would say to a person in that position. I would say that if you want to get better, you have to be bold. You have to make a decision to do something differently. I would say to stop working for someone else's goals and make a decision to start working for your own.

Everyone makes choices about what happens in their life. People might say that they didn't have a choice, when in reality, what they may have had was a very difficult choice. You've no doubt heard yourself or someone else say things like, "I have no choice but to work seventy hours a week" or "I have no choice but to continue working for someone else" or "I have no choice but to commute in rush-hour traffic every day." In such situations, "I have no choice" really means the choice is too difficult to make, or you want to pretend that it doesn't exist. That type of thinking can become a trap. You can pile one "no choice" on top of another until your life seems completely out of your control.

No matter where you are or what your situation, you do have a choice about almost everything you do. You have chosen the path you are on at the present and you have complete control over where you go in the future. Yes, the choices may indeed be difficult, but you will gain nothing by denying they exist. So, the next time you catch yourself saying "I have no choice," stop and ask yourself if it's really true. The more you make choices that move you in the direction of your objective, the faster you will arrive there.

DEFINE WHAT SUCCESS MEANS TO YOU

Almost everyone is obsessed with success, with having more money and more things, and with a better future for themselves and their family. Everyone is intrigued by the top companies, success stories of rags to riches, who's the coolest, the hottest, the richest, the boldest. But why is it that more people don't achieve great things? Instead, they just dream about it or stand on the sidelines observing other people's successes and justifying why they haven't been successful.

It's because most people have never defined what success would be for them, and they've never made a decision to have it. And that's the only reason! The most important question that you can ask yourself is, "Have I defined what success means to me or am I just working for someone else's success and letting them define my level of success?" How you answer that question can change your life.

So, your first step is to decide what it is you really want in your life. Do you want to be rich? Do you want to retire wealthy? You have to first define what success, what financial freedom means to you. Maybe it's having a secure job working for someone else, and if that's the case, that's okay. Someone has to build the cars, program the computers, and work in the salt mine. If no one is willing to do those jobs, we would have no salt on the table or cars to drive. Having a job and working for someone else is fine if that's what you love doing, but if not, stop right now and decide what it is you truly want.

What is success? It can be whatever you say it is, but you should define it just the same. It's not some goal defined by your parents, the media, or your friends. And if you measure success only in achievements made, milestones reached, money earned, or honors won, you will likely say one day, "Is that all there is?" But if you remain open to other possibilities, you can succeed in the most unexpected ways.

In order to define what success means to you, you might want to consider some of the following:

- Do you consider yourself a successful person?
- Do you think that others consider you successful?
- Do you have a success role model? If so, which of his or her attributes do you most admire—courage, personality, resourcefulness, self-confidence?
- Can you see any of these qualities in yourself?
- What is your definition of success?
- What behaviors, beliefs, or attitudes would you need to change to have success on your own terms?
- What one step could you take that would move you in the right direction?
- Do you need more money in order to live your definition of success?

For me, financial success represents personal freedom. It's not about the money, it's about being able to live my life on my own terms, to do what I want to do when I want to do it. So, if financial success represents personal freedom to you, my next question would be, "What does freedom mean to you?"

Once you've decided what it is you really want, the next step is to make a firm decision to have it. Now, for most of you, your mind will go to work and you will be thinking, "But how do I get it? What opportunity should I pursue? How will I know if I can really have it?" Forget all that! None of that matters right now.

Before you decide how you're going to do something, you have to first make a decision to have it. What you need to know, first and foremost, is where you want to go.

INTENTION AND VEHICLE

Let's do a little quiz. Two important components relating to your success are intention and vehicle. Intention is the decision you've made to be successful and the vehicle is the means you have chosen to get there. If their combined value represents 100 percent of your success, what percentage would each play in your success, in your attaining financial freedom? What do you think—50/50? I've heard people say 80/20, 20/80, 90/10, and so on, but seldom do I get the correct answer: It's 100 percent intention and 0 percent vehicle. But once the decision is made, then the vehicle becomes 100 percent as well. Because until you are 100 percent sure that you want what you want, and you have made a firm decision to have it, it doesn't matter what vehicle you choose, because no vehicle will make you successful until *you decide to become successful.*

Your firm decision to have what it is that you want creates a "mind-set." Your mind-set makes you as mechanical and predictable as a calculator—hit this number and it appears on the screen. It is absolutely essential to have a crystal clear picture of what you want to accomplish before you begin. If you want success, you must learn to operate with a sharply defined mental image of the outcome you want to attain. Focus your attention on the spot where you want to land, not on where you are now or on any misconceptions or shortcomings you may think you have. In other words, visualize your arrival. When you visualize your arrival, you develop a sort of magnetic harmony with the ways and means required to get there. You attract the people and circumstances needed to get where you want to go, solutions begin to appear and obstacles seem to disappear, and answers come to you.

If, however, you decide on the outcome you want and then start worrying about everything that will be involved in getting there, you'll just get bogged down in "mind chatter" and questions that have no answers. Most people get hung up on the unimportant things, like the "how to" aspects of getting where they want to go. If you have a strong vision or reason, then the answer, the vehicle, will come. And when the answer does appear, you will most likely find it to be a simple one.

Start by looking at your end result as something you are already prepared to do, but you just haven't done it yet. You have the potential, and the resources are available, to have anything you want. The only thing missing is your firm, unshakable decision to have it. Your success is something that you have been keeping from happening, it's not something you have to struggle to make happen. You can't force anything into existence—all you can do is step out of the way and let it happen. The key is to not let fear, doubt, mind chatter, or anything else stop you. By approaching success this way, the solutions taking you toward your goals will come to you in the most unexpected and sudden ways. You can never make something happen through struggle, but you can open yourself up and allow it to happen. Forcing something to happen takes an enormous amount of energy and time, while allowing it to happen takes almost none.

What I'm saying is that you don't need the "perfect plan" first. What you need is a perfectly clear decision about where it is you want to go, and the perfect plan to get you there will materialize.

HAVING A SUCCESS MIND-SET

Both failure and success are a mind-set. If you want to become a millionaire, you must first develop a "millionaire" mind-set. Your mind-set will determine what you do on a daily basis that "earns" you the right to success and financial freedom.

Let me tell you the exact point at which my success started. I was a factory worker on an assembly line. I had no money to start a business of my own and was living from paycheck to paycheck. I was a high school dropout, with no business background or experience at all. One of my co-workers asked me to attend a meeting one evening to take a look at a business opportunity. I asked him what it was all about and he said he didn't know, but he thought that we could both make some extra money. I gave him several excuses as to why I couldn't go, but then he said the magic words, "If you go with me, I'll buy you a beer after the meeting."

We arrived about fifteen minutes early. There were about forty people in attendance and the room was buzzing with excitement. Everyone was shaking hands with everyone else. I had never experienced this kind of enthusiasm. A little nervous and a bit skeptical, I sat in the back of the room and observed. As the meeting unfolded, I began to see what I believed to be an incredible opportunity, one where it didn't matter what my background or experience might be. I heard testimonies from people just like me who were succeeding big time!

About halfway through the final speaker's presentation, I said to myself, "I can do this." I wanted to stand up and shout! Just as the speaker was finishing, I changed my self-talk to "I'm going to do this and I am going to be successful at it!" It was like a light was switched on in my head—a success light. I made a decision right then that didn't allow for failure. Looking back, that night was the most meaningful moment in my career, when I decided that I could and would be successful.

Afterward, the man presenting the meeting walked straight to the back of the room, right up to me, and he asked, "Well, young man, do you see yourself being a part of this business?"

I said, "Yes, I sure do!"

He explained that I could get started in my own business in one of three ways. One would cost me $3, which I could afford. The next was for $300, which I could not afford. And the last was for $4,000, which was my income for about eighteen months at the factory. Enthusiastically, I told him that I was going to start at the $4,000 level. I had no idea where that answer came from or, for that matter, where the money was going to come from to get involved. All I knew was that this was the opportunity of a lifetime for me. I never once considered the risk. All I could see was a way out of the factory and, for the first time in my life, a way to build something for my future. I knew that the real risk was in *not* doing it, because I might not get another opportunity like this one.

He said, "Great, all I need is for you to fill out this application and attach a check for $4,000."

I explained that I didn't have the money, but that I would go to my bank (where I had a whopping nine dollars on deposit) the next day and get a loan. Over the next ten days, I applied for a loan at twenty-two different banks and loan companies, and all of them said "No!" One even said "No, not now, not ever," or something to that effect. I wouldn't give up, though. I had one place left to try, a transition place between the high interest rate loan companies and the Mafia. I gave the loan officer the most convincing story I could about my success with this new venture and told him that he was my last chance. Long story short, he made me the loan.

The next day, I quit my job and started my new business. After two weeks, a big truck pulled up in front of my home and unloaded about 8,000 bottles of soap, completely filling my double-car garage, with no room to spare. I was in business and I was excited about my future.

About two weeks later, I was informed by the company that I had met the necessary qualifications to move to the next position in their marketing plan. All I needed was another $4,000. I had no idea where I could come up with another $4,000, but my decision to be successful, which didn't allow for turning back, prevailed. I convinced my father-in-law to mortgage his dairy farm and loan me the money. After ten days, another big truck pulled up in front of my home and unloaded another 8,000 bottles of soap, this time into my house. My garage was still full from the first order, and now I had about 16,000 bottles of soap! Then, the only person I had introduced to the business received his first order. However, he had a one-car garage, a smaller home, and twelve kids who needed every inch of space in the house. When his wife came home and saw the soap, she said, in so many words, "Either the soap goes or you go." So, he gave me, for free, his 8,000 bottles of soap.

Now, I had 24,000 bottles of soap that almost filled my house.

I certainly knew at that point that I was in business—I was living in a warehouse! I needed to learn how to sell, so I borrowed some money from my brother and signed up for a Dale Carnegie sales class. I graduated at the top of the class. I was very good at selling. Over the next year, I sold my house, my car, my furniture—everything but my soap! Actually, I lost everything I owned. My home was in foreclosure and I was within five days of living on the street. I wouldn't give up though, because I was determined to make my business a success. I still did not waiver in my decision to be successful.

Everyone, including my father, tried to convince me to take back my old job at the factory. He said, "Son, you've got responsibilities. You have a family to look out for here."

I said, "I can't quit, I just can't. I am going to be a success in this business, no matter what."

That's a quick summation of my first year in the business. What happened next was almost unbelievable. Even after totally failing during my first year, within the next six months, I was earning ten times each month what I had been earning at the factory each year. Over the next few days, what I call a series of miracles took place. I had a car to drive, a place to live (complete with furniture), an income, a telephone that was no longer disconnected for non-payment, and I even had a place to store my soap!

The reason I succeeded was that I possessed the most vital ingredient for success. It's what kept me in the business even though, by all outward appearances, I had failed. It's called a "success mind-set." I had made a decision that very first night at the meeting to be successful. The "success light" went on and it was so bright that it couldn't go out, even though by all outward appearances, I had failed miserably. I had the mind-set necessary to succeed, a "never-give-up" attitude. Success starts with having that kind of mind-set, with making that firm of a decision. All the knowledge and all the skill training in this book won't hold any value if you don't have a success mind-set.

You can't get all the answers up front. The success formula isn't neatly organized, with everything in its proper place and sequence, and all the risks eliminated before you make the move. If you want to be a successful entrepreneur, you have to sometimes "shoot from the hip." You can't count on everything being in place before you make a move. Make a move and then let everything fall into place.

To be a successful entrepreneur, you must be willing to cope with confusion for a while, and shape your plan as you go. Allow some disorder, then create order out of it. If you get too detailed in the beginning, you'll find yourself worrying over potential problems, nonproductive details, instead of what's really important—getting the job done. All you'll need initially is a target point, then take action. Being a successful entrepreneur, by its very nature, means that you will have to move into unfamiliar, uncharted territory with no road map to follow. When you are going into new territory, you have to chart the map as you go. Hey, if it was easy, everybody would be doing it!

Having the right mind-set is the first ingredient in a formula for stunning advancement toward the realization of your dreams. It can let you take quantum leaps rather than incremental gains. It's like comparing addition to multiplication—which one will produce a larger number faster? Having the right mind-set will create geometric progression in your effectiveness, in what you attract, and in how you view the world. Even more importantly, how the world views *you* will change dramatically. Now, to me that's very exciting, even a bit mystical, but it can get even better. There are higher velocity moves in the formula that will even take you higher and faster, without the time-consuming struggle.

Here's my point once again: Your success is determined by *you,* by your method of thinking, your beliefs, and your behaviors. All of these factors make up your mind-set. Of course, many other factors will make a difference, but the number one factor that will determine your success is *you* and your *mind-set!* Nothing will produce any lasting success until you make a change in your mindset. If you want to become rich, you *must* have the mind-set of a rich person—it's as simple as that. Everything in your life is *exactly* as *you* pictured it to be, the result of your current and past mind-set.

The Master Switch

Someone once asked me how he could tell what his mind-set was toward money. I replied, "That's simple, just look in your bank account." If you don't like what you see, simply change your mind-set and everything else will follow. In fact, you can look at almost any area of your life—health, money, relationships—and tell what your mind-set is in that area. Try it; it's a real awakening exercise, a matter of being self-observant.

Turn on your "success light"—not the "positive thinking" light, or the "hope" light, or the "someday" light—I'm talking about the "master switch." Here's an example: Let's say that you've been saving to buy yourself a new Corvette. You had already picked all the options, the color, the customized wheels, and so on. That baby is loaded! It's the car of your dreams. You've made a decision to own one. The day arrives and you have the money you need. You head for the dealer, and you can smell the leather and feel the power of the engine as you accelerate even before you get there. In your mind, you already own that car and it's just a matter of going to the dealer and picking it up. But when you arrive, the dealer informs you that they are sold out of Corvettes and there are none to be had anywhere in the country. However, they have a real nice Chevette in the same color and you could own several for the price of one Corvette. Would you buy the Chevette? Of course not! That would not be an option, would it? Why not? Simple—you have a "Corvette mind-set" not a "Chevette mind-set." Chevettes are reserved for those who are not willing to make a decision, who settle for less. That's why they manufacture Chevettes!

Your mind-set determines how you show up. You can show up as a victim, unfocused, looking for what's wrong, looking for reasons why something won't work. A victim will read this book and think of all the reasons why the ideas could never work. A winner will read it looking for all the reasons it will work. A victim will settle for the Chevette just so he'll have something to complain about. A winner will settle for nothing less than what he or she wants.

I was recently in Santa Monica, California. It was a warm, sunny day and I had some time to relax, so I decided I would walk down the Third Street Promenade, an outdoor entertainment, shopping, and restaurant area near the beach. As I was walking, a young man caught my interest. He appeared to be homeless. He had ragged clothing, no shoes, and stringy hair, and smelled like he hadn't had a bath in months. As he walked about twenty feet ahead of me, he stopped at each trash receptacle, apparently looking for food. Suddenly, he pulled out a half-full bag of popcorn from the trash and began eating it. He took a few bites and stuffed the rest in his knapsack. He then looked into another trash receptacle, and pulled out a half-eaten hamburger, which he promptly devoured. As he walked further, he spotted a partial bottle of soda sitting on the curb near a light post, picked it up, and drank what was left.

I was amazed as I watched this young man. He looked healthy and certainly able to work if he wanted. Further along, he passed a sidewalk café. There was a table near the sidewalk that had not yet been cleared, and as he passed it he reached over the rail and grabbed a mug containing some beer. He quickly downed it, then reached across the rail again and grabbed a couple of biscuits and stuffed them in his knapsack.

I thought to myself. "He had a popcorn appetizer, a soda, a hamburger main course, a cocktail, and a doggie bag with biscuits to take home for later. I wonder what he's going to have for dessert?"

I stopped for a moment and tried to put myself into his mind-set, but even imagining the very worst situation I could ever be in, I couldn't for the life of me go there. I thought, "Okay, I am bankrupt and have no money. Could I do what he is doing?" I still couldn't go there. I would come up with a way to make money. My mind-set wouldn't allow me to mentally go there, it was not a part of my consciousness. I'm not saying that he was right or wrong. He is what he is. It's just that we all do what we do, and have what we have, because of our mind-set. It's as simple, and as complex, as that!

If you show up looking like a victim, people treat you like one, and with that, you'll end up a victim. On the other hand, if you show up to win and nothing else will do but winning, people will treat you like a winner and you'll end up winning. In other words, by making a firm decision to be successful and financially free, you have ruled out everything but that result. If you have a failure mind-set, what you have done is ruled out success. Financial freedom and success begin and end with your mind-set, with your decision to be financially free. In order to be successful, you have to turn on the light, the "master switch," to see the way.

DON'T LISTEN TO POVERTY-MINDED PEOPLE

This world is changing, and if you want freedom you have to change with it. If you want to be successful, you cannot allow unsuccessful people to influence you. If people would just open their minds and change some of the ways they look at things and not listen to poverty-minded people, they might see the value in the risk of doing what they want. I want my freedom and I'm willing to do whatever it takes to have it. And that includes making my own decisions about what I do or don't do, whether my friends or business associates agree with me or not. It's okay to listen, but I only take advice from an expert.

Freedom, to me, simply means that you have more choices. But in order to have freedom, you have to develop a freedom mind-set. You have to choose freedom. If you have a job, you've probably given up a lot of your freedom. Somebody tells you how much money you make, when you come to work, when you eat lunch, when you go home, when you get a pay raise, and even when to retire. I'm not interested in having somebody tell me how much money I can make or whether I have a job tomorrow or not. Having the right mind-set is the first step to becoming the "game maker" instead of a pawn in someone else's game.

CREATE YOUR OWN PATH TO SUCCESS

The idea of moving more quickly to much higher achievement levels, and skipping several slow-moving steps along the way, may strike you as far-fetched or a bit outrageous. Taking the faster approach to achievement typically will not appear to you as the obvious move at the moment, but looking back, you will probably see the hidden logic behind your move. Don't get me wrong—making huge advancements quickly does not necessarily require complex or intricate maneuvers. Rather, they tend to be more energy and time efficient.

If you want to survive today, you have to be bold, and the first step is to reclaim your own freedom. You must be willing to make a radical departure away from some of your old habits and actions. If you want to be successful today, not only do you have to be emotionally strong, you need to make your own decisions and stand firm. People are financially poor because they let someone else make their decisions—they buy into the wrong plan. So, it is important to make the decision yourself and create the mind-set necessary to succeed. That's your first step to success.

YOU MUST HAVE TRUST AND FAITH

You have to trust in yourself and the decisions you make, and then you need to have faith that something bigger than you will appear to support you in your endeavor. You may call it the subconscious, the superconscious, the source, the universe, coincidence, luck, the hidden force, God, Buddha, or whatever you choose to call it. It doesn't really matter—have faith that the answers to your questions, the solutions to your problems, the contacts you need, whatever it may be that you need to fulfill your dream, will come when the time is right.

Moving quickly and effortlessly toward your desired outcome is merely a process of using yourself and the world in a different way than what you are accustomed to doing. It requires allowing other new possibilities to exist. Even more than that, you must allow them to materialize. A willingness to have faith in outside support will become your enabler. You must realize that you don't achieve your full potential and your dreams through your own efforts alone. Sheer willpower is not the answer, and trying harder will not take you as far as you are capable of going. If you want to attain the success you desire faster, you must take advantage of the support system that you cannot see.

Look at it as being in partnership. You provide the questions that need answers and the vision of where you want to go, and your invisible partner, the unseen power, will provide the answers. Have faith and you will begin to see amazing things happen. The unseen force will operate through your intuition and will materialize in what seems to be "luck" or some sort of mystical phenomenon. You've no doubt experienced it: You are suddenly hit with an answer to a difficult problem in a moment of solitude, or a solution may come to you in a dream or just as you are awakening, while all is quiet and you are relaxed. You have a flash of inspiration while you are mowing the grass and not thinking about business at all. You want to call someone and you can't locate their number and suddenly you get a call from that person. We've all had that sort of thing happen, and passed it off as a mere coincidence. Again, call it what you want or just accept it as a coincidence, it doesn't matter. Just accept it and know that there is more where that came from.

It's important to have a clear vision of what you want, otherwise these unseen forces will operate in confusion, bringing you more confusion. Know exactly what you want and communicate it clearly so that you receive the correct support. Remember, you will gain support for whatever it is you communicate. That can be exciting or scary, depending on your point of view.

If you just back away and observe, you will be dazzled with what happens, and the impact it will have on your success and your life. And you can count on it. You don't even have to understand it, just plug in with your faith. Know that it is there, stay clear about where you want to go, and watch it work for you. You don't have to understand how a radio wave works to tune into a certain station, do you? All you have to do is get good at tuning into the right station, and it sends out the correct signal so that you receive the music you want. You always get back what you put out. The question you should ask yourself often is, "What signal am I sending out?" Of course, that's easy to know—just look at what you are receiving, and you'll know exactly what frequency you're on.

USING YOUR IMAGINATION

Do not approach your business casually, because a casual approach will always produce casualties. What you can accomplish is limited only by your imagination. Financial security is not something that will simply happen to you one day. It is created and achieved on purpose through consistent actions toward well-defined objectives. What sets us apart from the other species of animals on the planet is our ability to imagine. Your true greatness lies within your imagination. Decide what you want, make a commitment to have it, and then imagine it into existence.

For example, suppose that you set out to start your own retail business. You certainly want to be successful. You have purchased your inventory of merchandise to stock your shelves, and you've invested a sizeable amount of money to do so. Next, you open your doors and offer your merchandise for sale, but no one comes in to buy your product, and so you make no sales. And the overhead just keeps on going. The "mind chatter" starts. Your immediate thought is that you've made a serious mistake and that you are going to lose all your money. And before long, if you don't change your way of thinking, you become convinced that your business is doomed to fail. You begin to visualize it and may even see yourself going bankrupt. You lose all hope and see yourself as a victim of cruel fate.

Think about that situation. How would you react? Would you be convinced that you were going to be a success or would you be convinced you were going to fail? Chances are that a large part of your attention might be focused on possible failure. And as long as failure is predominant in your mind, you most likely would eventually fail. A feeling of success or failure will always back your every action. The feeling you hold becomes a magnet, attracting supporting circumstances. That feeling is one of the major reasons that new businesses fail. The business owner hasn't developed the mental toughness to stick with his or her attitude of success when things are going wrong.

If you want success, you have to refuse to accept your circumstances as a mistake or a failure. Positive thinking alone or hoping the problem will simply go away are not enough. Rather, have the understanding that if you remain in a resourceful place, and stay focused on the end result, a solution will present itself. Don't get me wrong—if there's a problem that needs handling, don't just say, "I have faith that it will go away." You still have to deal with the problems at hand, but you do so by looking for a solution, not by being blinded by the problem. Dealing with and solving problems is part of the refining process toward success. The key is where your focus lies.

You are in business to solve problems—that's the nature of business. The problem is that you don't have any customers, or that you need a higher return on your investment, or that you don't have the right team members to take your business to the next level. Your job is to find a solution to the problems, not to focus on them. When you focus on the problems, you can't see a way past them. Move forward with a resourceful attitude about your success. When you truly understand that success is a state of mind, not just an outcome, any moment can be a victory. The real problem is not what is happening to us, but rather our worries about what we think should be happening or not happening. If we always aspire to victory, those worries disappear.

Imagine taking a picture with your (non-digital) camera. You have it in focus, perfectly framed for the perfect shot, and you snap the shutter. Then, right after you take the shot, you open up the camera and look at the film to see if it came out all right. You wouldn't do that, would you? The same should apply to your vision. You create the vision, get it into clear focus, then you snap it by saying, "Yes, that's what I want to accomplish." Then, trust in the process while dealing with the problems along the way.

In every failure there lies a greater opportunity. When you move forward with complete conviction, you find a market for your goods, created perhaps from a totally different market than what you originally envisioned. I know a man who developed a product and was determined to sell it through retail drugstores. After several years without much success, instead of giving up, he proceeded ahead, knowing there was a way to make his product a success. A short time later, he met someone who wanted to market it on television in an infomercial. Within two years, he had made a profit of nearly $100 million!

DON'T EVER GET IN THE BOX

You've no doubt heard the saying, "Think outside the box." Here's a much better way of looking at it: "Don't ever get in the box."

The world you perceive is the world you will create. And *the world you create is limited only by your imagination and your conviction.* Your world is, and will be, a reflection of the vision you choose for your life, whether or not you have made a conscious decision regarding that vision. Your conviction regarding that vision decides the quality of your life and your degree of success. Indecision attracts confusion, while decision attracts structure that moves you toward your objective. Begin to focus on what you want to accomplish and then move forward with complete confidence that the accomplishment is yours. By doing that, you are allowing it to materialize and take form in your life rather than trying to force your accomplishment into existence.

Which sounds like the better approach: to *attack* your goals and dreams or to *attract* your goals and dreams? You make the choice by either focusing on the problem or on the solution to the problem. You attract what you want and need by having faith that success will be your eventual outcome.

4

Eliminate Time Constraints

What's the difference between someone who earns $100,000 a year and someone who earns $1,000,000 a year, other than $900,000? Does he or she work harder? Is the million-dollar earner smarter? Not necessarily intellectually, but certainly with the use of time and energy. Everyone has about 24 hours a day from which to carve out his or her life, so what's the difference? It can only be a result of what they do with the time they have, how they "spend" their day.

Accelerated income growth cannot be achieved through incremental steps of doing "more of the same." If you want to move forward quickly, you have to shift into overdrive, into a pattern of new thoughts, beliefs, and actions. Think about it—more of the same can only produce more of the same. Change a little in the right direction and you achieve a little change; change a lot and you get lots of change.

Try harder and you can expect better results, right? Well, possibly to some degree, but not always. Sooner or later you are going to reach a point where you just can't work any harder. There are no more hours in the day and you are stretched to the limit both physically and mentally. You reach a point where your personal output becomes your downfall and trying harder and harder produces less and less. Increased personal efforts can even produce more and bigger problems, like stress, burnout, or marital difficulties.

I'm not saying that you don't need to have persistence or self-discipline. You need both, and they both can contribute greatly to your success. In fact, it would be hard to have any degree of success without both, because discipline and staying power are essential to producing a successful outcome. More times than not, though, you will find that simply trying harder will only produce incremental gains, not massive success. Trying to succeed by relying just on committed effort will only produce more of the same and can blind you to seeing a better, more efficient path to success.

So, if you want more, if you want to move to higher levels of achievement, more effort is not the answer. What is the answer? How can you make the changes needed to win the relentless competition against the clock? Does it take a miracle to stop the clock long enough to give you a chance to play "catch up"?

THE SECRETS OF MAXIMUM PERSONAL PRODUCTIVITY

I am convinced that everybody can unlock the secrets of maximum personal productivity. I am convinced that everybody can dramatically improve their life, achieve greater financial rewards, and still have more time to enjoy life. Everybody can make his or her dreams come true, sooner rather than later.

Two things are essential: the *will* to make a change and the *skill* to become smarter about the use of your time. You can't stop the clock, but you can learn new skills that will allow you to harvest more of what you want in less time. You can become "result oriented" instead of "effort oriented." I'm going to offer you a simple system to follow that, when used daily, will absolutely "turbo charge" your performance. It will show you how to take a broader view of everything you do, to look at your day from a whole different perspective.

Time, as we commonly know it, exists in three forms: past, present, and future. The past is the time we've already spent, the future represents "unused time," and the present is where everything happens. But every second that passes represents one less you have left.

Let's look at this in the context of performance. Your past can be an incredible learning resource. Maybe you have discovered something or developed some skill that has worked for you in the past and you can now utilize that same skill to repeat the same actions again. You don't have to relearn the skill all over again. In a case where you may have gained less than favorable results, you can use that experience to adjust future actions to avoid repeating the same mistakes. In both cases, the past can be of great value to you.

However, none of us can go back and change the result that has already occurred. We can't push "rewind" and do it over again. It does not matter if something happened three years, three months, three hours, or three minutes ago, there is nothing you can do now to change the results you produced in the past, no matter how hard you try. The only value the past has for you now is the knowledge and skills gained from the time you've invested acquiring the experience. It's like learning the skill of driving a car. You don't have to relearn it every time you get behind the wheel. You don't have to get in and say, "Now I wonder how to drive this thing?"

The future, on the other hand, is yet to be determined and is comprised of an unlimited universe of possibilities. Any of these possible futures is where your "someday" dreams, goals, and strategies will be made real, or not. Only time will tell just which possible future will become *your* reality. Time *and* your performance, that is—because when it comes to determining which of the alternative futures actually becomes your reality, it will be your performance right now, in this passing moment, that makes all the difference. There is absolutely nothing you can do, no matter how hard you try, to alter the past; and there is nothing you can do about future results that do not yet exist. What you can do, however, is make corrections to improve your actions and performance right now.

FIFTEEN-MINUTE BLOCKS

Becoming more effective with your time is really quite simple—it's realizing that your ability to cause something to occur, from the inception to the completion of a task to the realization of your dreams, can only happen at this moment in time. If you can perform better right now, the future automatically becomes better, doesn't it? And your actions, your performance, your aspirations, and intention to be a success is what molds the future into what you want.

When you begin to work smarter, you will gain unlimited power over your performance *right now,* which will deliver to you all your hopes and dreams, sooner rather than later. Again, there are just twenty-four hours in each day. Do rich people get more than their share? Is there more time allotted to people with certain talents and abilities? We all have the same amount of time—1,440 minutes each day to spend any way we choose. If you subtract roughly five hundred minutes for sleep, you are left with about nine hundred minutes in which all your dreams will become realized, or they won't.

To get an even clearer picture, try this: divide your day, the nine hundred minutes, into fifteen-minute blocks of time. That's sixty blocks. Your fifteen-minute blocks of time begin ticking away the second you jump out of bed in the morning. If you hit the fifteen-minute snooze alarm, there goes one block, and you now have fifty-nine left. You spend one fifteen-minute block after another, from the beginning to the end of your day. The question is, how are you spending them?

In my first experiment with counting time, I decided to track where I spent my time for an entire month. If you want an awakening, try doing that! Every fifteen minutes, write down what you did for the last block of time. Shower, shave, and get dressed, three blocks. Eat breakfast, thirty minutes, two blocks of time spent. Drive to the office, thirty minutes, another couple of fifteen-minute blocks. Watch television for two hours, that's eight blocks spent.

I remember having a two-hour business lunch that was completely nonproductive. As I wrote it down on the calendar as eight fifteen-minute blocks, it was a rude awakening. I could have accomplished the same result by spending only one fifteen-minute block of time or with a quick telephone call. I could have saved myself an hour and forty-five minutes for something more productive. I suddenly got a totally different view of my day and why I had a problem getting all the things done that I wanted to do. Once you become aware that the fifteen-minute blocks are ticking away day after day, the question becomes, what are you going to do with each block?

This is a very different view of your day from the traditional time planners and appointment schedules. What you have here is a countdown clock that starts when you get up in the morning, and runs out when you go to bed about sixty blocks of time later. And there is nothing you or anyone else can do to gain back even one minute from your countdown clock. When your nine hundred minutes are over, they're over; when each fifteen-minute block is over, it's over. The question is, "What did you do with your last one?" And, more importantly, what are you going to do with your next one? Learn from your last fifteen-minute block. And if you stop to regret how you spent your last block, wishing you'd done it differently, you are only wasting the next block of time. So, don't spend *any* time regretting mistakes, move on! It's over! Next!

When you begin to break down your day into "bite-sized" portions, you become aware of your performance in the present, right now, which is all you have anyway. I call these fifteen-minute bite-sized portions "power points." When you look at your day in this way, you no longer lose hours of time and wonder where they went. You now have sixty chances to put forth your best efforts and to gain more rewards sooner! You also have sixty chances, sixty power points, to make corrections to your actions and improve your performance. You are now in total control of the present moment, where the real action is taking place. And if you find yourself off track, you can quickly move in the right direction toward your desired outcome. Plan for the future, yes, but stay focused on the present moment.

Try this exercise for the next week or so, and watch how your performance immediately improves. Every fifteen minutes, stop for a moment and ask yourself, "Did my actions during the last fifteen minutes move me closer to my desired results, and if not, why not?" If not, what can you do differently that will move you in the right direction faster?

The reality is that people can't perform at their optimum level and achieve the success they want without first doing something about their fifteen-minute blocks of time. And fifteen minutes is the perfect slot of time, the right-sized power point, because it's enough time for you to do something significant toward your success. And it's short enough that if you find yourself moving away from your objective, you can correct your actions before you waste a lot of time going the wrong way. There's nothing worse, in my thinking, than discovering at the end of your day that you have been moving really fast in the wrong direction. We all do it, and in this busy world it is easy to do without realizing what is happening.

Everyone is efficient in what they do some of the time. But the fact is that if you could be more efficient with even a single fifteen-minute block each day, your life would be better, your capacity to create would be increased, and you'd have more time to focus on the things most important to you. Gaining fifteen minutes each day can be very powerful. In fact, over the course of a year, you would gain an extra ninety-one hours. That's over two working weeks! What if you improved ten of your power points? What about all sixty? What if you saved yourself an hour in each workday? That's more than eight forty-hour work weeks in a year. What could you do with those extra weeks each year—get rich, enjoy life more, take an extended vacation, produce more?

When you become more observant of your actions, the time you spend on them, and the results you are actually producing, you will be able to improve your performance at will. This method of increasing your performance means that you will never again take for granted any fifteen-minute block of time. Observe yourself periodically throughout the day and ask yourself, "Right now, am I producing the results that I'm capable of getting with the time I'm investing?" It's this sort of continuous monitoring of your progress that will make you more efficient about everything you do and about the results you produce. And after you apply this method of self-observation for a while, it will become second nature, a habit.

Knowing clearly where you are going, having a clear vision of success, and knowing where you are at any given time allows you to have a constant reading on both your direction and your speed toward your objective. The following are what I call *"time power points"* that will help you in becoming more efficient with your time and allow you to perform at your peak.

ENERGY GAINERS, ENERGY DRAINERS

There's nothing worse, when you want to get things done, than to be too tired to think and perform efficiently. Peak performance requires a high level of energy, and high energy requires a total commitment to being fit and healthy. By putting more energy into what you do, you will automatically get more results in less time.

Most people spend their younger years trying to accumulate wealth, then later in life they spend their wealth trying to regain their health. The sad truth is that most people take better care of their car than they do their own bodies. They feed their dog better than they do themselves and they maintain their homes better than they maintain their health! It's amazing to me what some people put into their bodies on a regular basis, and then complain that they get sick or too tired to perform the way they want.

I made a decision about thirty years ago that I was going to be a healthy person, that taking care of my health was going to be a priority for me from that point forward. What is the most important thing to you in life? You might say, money, family, etc., but when it really comes down to it, feeling good should be at the top of the list. The problem is that most people put it at the bottom of their list until they get sick. Keep this in mind: You will always endure one of two pains in life, the pain of discipline or the pain of regret. The pain of discipline weighs ounces, while the pain of regret can weigh tons. The discipline it takes to stay healthy and keep your energy at its optimum will reap tremendous rewards, and they will be immediate!

I'm not a trained nutritionist, but I do know a lot about the subject. To me, the body is pretty simple. Its natural state is health. Let me put it another way—*your health is a gift and disease is something you earn.* You don't "catch" a disease. Whether you get cancer, a headache, the flu, or anything else, you give it to yourself through lack of doing the necessary things to stay healthy. If you experience ongoing fatigue, midday energy slumps, headaches, cloudy thinking, memory recall problems, or crave stimulants like caffeine, sugar, and cigarettes, then you probably suffer from a nutritional deficiency.

In order to gain a high level of performance, you must rid yourself of *energy drainers* and replace them with *energy gainers,* like "live" nutritionally rich food and a daily exercise program. Drinking a cup of coffee is an energy drainer. It may feel at the time like an energy gainer, but there's a letdown later. Taking a short walk during the day is an energy gainer. Eating refined foods like breakfast cereal is an energy drainer; eating fresh fruits is an energy gainer. Eating fast foods or a heavy meal for lunch is an energy drainer; eating a salad for lunch is an energy gainer. Alcohol for lunch is an energy drainer; fresh-squeezed juice is an energy gainer.

If you want to operate at peak performance, you must ruthlessly eliminate anything that drains your energy and replace it with something that provides energy. Your body is constantly burning nutrients. If these are not replenished regularly, then the cells within your body begin to slow down and die. The results are a slower thinking process, lack of energy, and the inability to function efficiently, and eventually this leads to degeneration and disease—one that you've given yourself. Most people have grown to accept this as just a normal part of life—eat poorly, have low energy, get tired, and perform poorly—when, in fact, it is not normal at all, but it is common. Accomplishing uncommon goals requires being an uncommon person, and to do that requires having an uncommon level of energy and vitality.

Just remember, if your body fails you for an hour, a day, or longer, you're out of the game for that period of time. Peak performance requires a commitment to renewing your energy on a continuous basis. And if you are not aware of how much energy you are *draining* and what's causing the drainage, and how much energy you are *gaining* and what you are doing to gain it, chances are you'll run out of energy long before your nine hundred minutes run out each day.

KNOW YOUR MISSION

What's your mission? This will be a critical component to the success of your business. Until you know where you're going, you won't even know when you get there. You may be spending all your time on things that don't even matter. If you lack direction and purpose in your business, you are absolutely powerless to make any real progress. However, all self-imposed limitations will begin to melt away when your mind and heart are focused on the same thing with a clear vision and a mission for success. You will always be operating at your "point of power" when you tap into the unlimited power generated by working from your heart's desire and fulfilling a clearly defined mission.

To clarify your mission, begin to search your heart and mind for what means the most to you. Is it integrity, contribution to others, peace of mind, freedom, financial freedom, being your own boss? These become your core values and the by-products of building your successful business that will bring you the greatest sense of satisfaction. This becomes the driving force behind your business.

Next, put in writing, very succinctly, your mission statement, outlining what you'll do to operate within these values all the time. For example, if one of your values is to always provide the best quality product with the best ingredients, when you find yourself beginning to add things of less quality because it costs you less, you'll know you have gone against your core values. If one of your core values is to always provide the best customer service and you find that you no longer listen to what your customers want, you are going against your core values. Write your mission statement as your code of conduct or ethics, which will lead you directly toward what you want to experience. When you have a set of values to live by and from which to run your business, you'll find decisions that you wrestled with before become easy and simple to make, saving you an enormous amount of time in the process.

Your vision is simply a very clear, highly compelling, mental image of your ideal outcome. Your mission is how you plan to get there, with your core values as the guidelines by which you operate your life and your business, how you arrive at your vision. Both are absolutely critical to getting the most out of your nine hundred minutes each day. And if you go against your core values, you'll sabotage your own success. If you don't ever stop to decide just what your values are, what's really most important to you, you'll spend a great deal of your day chasing things that have little, if any, bearing on your success. By creating a compelling vision and mission for yourself and your business, and identifying your core values—what you want to accomplish and why, and what you will do to get there—you give *direction* and *purpose* to every task at every moment during your day.

SET CLEAR OBJECTIVES

Your objectives directly relate to getting more done in less time. A goal is simply a vision with a deadline, a target for future accomplishments. Plus, the first step in *getting* what you want is to decide *exactly* what it is you want. To succeed at anything, you must have a vision to succeed and tangible targets that give you immediate direction. Then, you must have a strategy for specific actions.

Unclear goals give you nothing to aim at and, therefore, you won't know if your accomplishments today are taking you where you want to go. Your goals are simply the milestones, the step-by-step strategies, to accomplish your vision. When you picture how you want your ideal world to look, your goals simply provide the strategies you will need to get there. Only when you are clear about what you want can you identify when you are on the right track. In other words, by having clear objectives, you'll know exactly where you *are* on your road to success. And when you reach each milestone along the way, it can and will inspire you to the next one and the next.

Years ago, at a seminar on success, I met an eight-year-old boy who was attending with his mother. When asked what he got out of the seminar, he said, "I learned that goals are things people get and that wishes are for poor people." Even he realized that you can't wish your way to success—you have to strategize your way there. And you have to become 100 percent personally responsible for making your goals a reality.

To be at your most productive, set specific objectives and then hold yourself accountable for accomplishing them. I'm not talking about pie-in-the-sky goals, I'm talking about clear strategies that will move you toward your vision. Remember, whether you choose your goals carelessly or with great care, you are always on the road to accomplishing them. If you are not committed to a clearly defined outcome, then you will simply end up with whatever life chooses to give you, your goal by default.

Having a plan to accomplish your goal is critical. You'll want to develop a business plan with specific steps to implement each new project. In other words, plan your steps before you take them. Where are you and where do you want to go? How do you plan on getting there? Of course, your plans may change as you go, and sometimes rapidly, but your goal remains the same. And if your plan must change, if you hit a detour or a road block, you simply map out new precise steps to get there.

Create your plan by beginning with the end in mind and take the shortest path to get there. "How do I get there? What do I do first, second, and so on?" If you don't know, ask for some professional help. Study the industry or find someone that is already successful or has some professional experience in your chosen business and ask them for advice.

A Case Study

Years ago, I learned about a particular type of test that measured the reaction of white blood cells to over two hundred different types of foods. The objective of the test was to discover what foods might not be compatible or might be contributing to certain health conditions. Being very entrepreneurial minded, when I learned about the test, I said to the woman who introduced it to me, "Now that's saleable!" I thought that everyone could benefit from knowing the results of this procedure and decided that I was going to market this procedure in some way.

The next day, I set out to find someone who performed the test and I found a small laboratory in Northridge, California, about fifty miles from where I lived. It was a small operation and the owners had no ambitions for getting any larger. I decided to go to the source and find the person who manufactured the actual test kits for the procedure. After two days, I found him in the same county where I was living and set up a luncheon appointment for the next day. During lunch, I told him my plan for marketing this test: to set up clinics around the country and offer this program along with a complete medical work-up and a follow-up nutritional program for treatment. Medical doctors would perform the actual test and nutritionists would do the treatment program through dietary recommendations and nutritional supplements.

He said, "Let me save you a lot of time and money. I tried to set up a clinic like that in San Francisco a couple of years ago and it failed miserably. In one year, I did a grand total of $1,600 in business. So, as good as it looks, it won't work."

I looked him straight in the eye and said, "What does your lack of success have to do with me succeeding?" You see, he had decided to "give it a try," whereas I decided to make it a successful business. He also didn't have the strategy plan that I had in mind to bring customers in the door.

Before the end of our lunch, he said to me, "I believe that you might make this work."

I said, "I don't 'believe' that I am going to make it work, I *know* I am!"

He was so taken by my response that he said, "Do you need a partner? I would be open to funding the whole project as well as providing you with the test kits." So, we formed a partnership and opened our first clinic about six weeks later. In the first month, we were in the black with sales that exceeded $80,000. By the end of the first year, we had one million dollars in the bank and had opened four clinics.

It started with a clear vision and a clear intention to succeed. I had a mission to change the way people cared for their health, to get people to take more responsibility for their own well-being. I knew clearly what I wanted to do, I knew there was a need for what I wanted to offer, and I had a clear plan for an initial starting point.

My first goal was to open a clinic and develop a prototype that I could duplicate, but I had to get people in the door. Some of the strategies I planned to apply to make my clinic successful were:

- Newspaper and magazine advertising
- A referral program from satisfied existing customers
- A doctor referral program
- Seminars, where past satisfied customers could invite their friends to hear about the program
- Newspaper articles and press releases
- Direct mail and direct response

But I couldn't do everything at once, so I had to decide which method of marketing would launch my business the fastest, with the least amount of risk and the most amount of exposure. Then, I had to determine the sequence of marketing concepts I would implement.

I started with a newspaper advertisement, which I thought would be the best approach and get the quickest response for the least money. I wrote the ad myself and placed it in the *Los Angeles Times* on a Sunday in the main news section. It would get the greatest amount of exposure in that section because almost everyone reads the main news. By Monday morning when we opened the office, our message machine was already full with dozens of calls. The telephone didn't stop ringing all day and into the night. It was so successful that it would have been very easy to just forget the rest of the marketing plan.

I also suspected that eventually the "new" might wear off with the newspaper advertisment and it might not be as effective in the future. So, my next plan was to implement a satisfied patient referral program, which I called the "Tell-a-Friend" program. People were getting such good results that they were telling all their friends about it. The program sold for about five hundred dollars and it cost me about one hundred in advertising dollars to get a new client. The referral program gave each new client a fifty-dollar discount that could be applied to the program and the referring client got a fifty-dollar gift certificate that could be redeemed at the clinic for nutritional supplements and other services. This promotion also worked great.

KNOW YOUR NEXT SHOT

I always apply to my business strategies what my dad taught me about playing pool—play "position." When playing position, you don't just plan your next shot, you plan your next three, four, or five shots, as many as possible. And you do this before you take the next shot. You should always be thinking, "What's next?"

You must take the time to think and plan ahead. Any project you have, regardless of how big it is, becomes nothing more than a series of well-planned future steps leading to your desired outcome. If one step doesn't work, you simply take another until you find what works. As it turned out, every one of the initial marketing strategies I started with worked. Some better than others, but they all worked to one degree or another. Later, I tried some new things that didn't work, and when I discovered that a certain strategy didn't work, I simply didn't do it anymore.

Every strategy, whether it works or not will always lead you to the next step and eventually to your ultimate goal. Just remember, don't get yourself bogged down in what didn't work. A plan is not set in concrete. Your decision to be successful is set in concrete, but the plan to get there is always evolving and changing. Find what works and do more of it; discover what doesn't work and quickly eliminate it.

Just because you have your plan completed, it still remains to be implemented. Creating a red hot exciting plan and then spending the day sitting on your sofa reviewing it is called a "red hot poor person." You've got to implement the plan in order to get a result, positive or negative. By scheduling each step of your plan into specifics—when you know what you are going to do today—you create the "structural tension" necessary to lead you to your desired outcome for that day. What you do on a daily basis that "earns" you the right to success is where your goals and plans meet with action and your actions meet with results.

Your awareness of the importance of having a clear plan to start is critical to getting the results you desire and to getting the most out of your nine hundred minutes each day. Without a clear plan, you'll continually find yourself stuck in nonproductive places and situations where you have no interest in being in the first place. When you have a plan, you'll get more of the results you aspire to, with fewer wasted steps and in a shorter period of time.

ATTITUDE IS EVERYTHING

Your attitude is your mind-set for success. It will open up the flow for the correct sequence of events to take place in order to move you toward your objective. Your attitude will turn your vision, goals, and plans into sheer power. Everyone has the same nine hundred minutes and your attitude will determine how many opportunities come your way as well as which ones you'll recognize and transform into results.

You may have a real passion for success, but until you develop the attitude that what you are doing is going to *be* a success no matter what, nothing happens. Which of the following words do you think is stronger—*hope, think, try, believe,* or *know?*

Hope means "to entertain an outcome."

Think is defined as "to contemplate."

Try means "to struggle."

Believe is defined as "to hold an opinion."

Know means "to be certain."

When asked, most people will say that *believe* is the strongest word. Do you "believe" your business will be a success or do you "know" it will be? Certainty is the place to start. Forget belief—all beliefs are limiting. Bypass belief and get to "knowing," to being certain. When asked if I believed that my clinic concept would work, I said, "No, I don't 'believe' it will work, I *know* it will work." Belief is in your head and knowing is from your heart. When you connect your head with your heart, things really start to happen. Your decision is in your heart and your plan is in your head. Connect your head with your heart!

When you connect the vision in your mind to your heart, it creates passion, and miracles happen. Nothing will ever be produced of any significance until your *knowing* is strong enough to transform your passion into action. In order to reach maximum productivity, you've got to know that you know—your mind and heart must enthusiastically agree and say, "Yes, this is it. Let's go!"

Whether or not you transform your passion into action and your action into results is a delicate balance between the clarity of your objective and your determination to not allow distractions pull you away from the desired outcome. If you are not operating from a level of complete certainty, distractions and those "silent whispers" in your own mind can rob you of valuable time as well as your dream.

If you convince yourself that your actions will never succeed, or that the reward for your efforts may be failure, you simply won't put forth the necessary effort to make it happen. Without an aspiring attitude, at best you will proceed cautiously, with minimum efforts, and you'll waste too much time and energy on something that isn't going to succeed in the first place. This can become a self-fulfilling prophecy of making things worse than they are. If you are not playing full out, you will always be looking for the reasons why it's not working instead of looking for ways to make it work. So, if you find yourself thinking or saying, "Why do others make it and I don't?" or "Why is this not working?" stop and change your focus to "How do I make this work?" and "How do I get rich?"

When you know that you have total control over your own future, because you know you have total control over the present moment, you can change the course of your direction in a heartbeat! When you fully know in your heart that your actions are going to pay off in a big way, you will automatically proceed with determination, and success will be yours. The stronger your knowing is toward your success, the more you'll perceive the potential reward. And the more you understand your potential reward, the greater is your desire to take action sooner!

You will enthusiastically take the next step, feeling fully empowered to move forward with every task, to take every project to completion, and to move forward until your goal is attained. Your attitude says, "I promise myself I will do whatever it takes to succeed. I can and I will, and won't it be wonderful when I do?" In fact, that would be a great success mantra. That's called a mind-set, an attitude.

If you don't think you can, you probably won't. However, when you are passionate and proactive, you will get the result you aspire to and it will come sooner rather than later. Your willingness to take action, to make full use of your time at that moment, gives you power over any situation that you may face and the best use of your nine hundred minutes each day.

SETTING PRIORITIES

By setting priorities, you can stay focused on your most important objectives. One of the ways you achieve maximum productivity is by making the right choices by focusing on what's "goal achieving" instead of "tension relieving." It's easy to get caught up in doing things that make you "feel" busy but have very little bearing on accomplishing your goals, or focusing on smaller goals that are easier to achieve but are of little importance.

Often, we have so many things to do that we attempt to do them all at once, which is a fatal mistake. Prioritizing is the key. Getting the most out of your time means making intelligent, conscious choices—deciding what can be done and what can wait. It's making intelligent choices that take you where you want to go, not making choices of convenience that are easier but less productive. It's having the self-discipline to put everything else on hold to focus on what is the most important to get done *now.*

Time and energy are wasted when you focus on things that don't really matter but that seem more urgent. When you take this approach, you may completely overlook what's really important. "Urgent" doesn't necessarily mean important. The real key is to know exactly what you want and which task is the most important at that point in time in getting there. Only when you know your mission, your vision, and your values can you then know the priority of each task at hand. Choosing can become natural if you compare your core values to your vision and then to each task at hand. The point is that your core values must become the determining factor in deciding what is the most important thing to do at any given time, and then, secondly, whether or not that action is leading you closer to your objective.

This may sound too simple, but it works. It will be the key to your success. The fact is that the list of core values you wrote while creating your mission statement is the most important list to carry with you. Once your core values are ingrained upon your mind and heart, knowing what to do at any given moment will become second nature.

Prioritizing means "to choose." First, choose what you want to accomplish—your vision, your mission, and your core values. Second, choose your goals—how you will get where you want to go, what incremental milestones will you reach and when. Third, choose the strategies, or tasks, that will move you toward your goals. As soon as you begin to make conscious, intelligent choices as to which goals and actions are most important, which ones are going to lead you to accomplishing more of your core values, you will automatically begin to focus on those things that are both *most important* as well as *most rewarding.*

Once you determine in advance what efforts will reap the greatest rewards, you will be prioritizing your tasks, not on the urgency of the day but on what will profoundly help you to achieve your desired outcome. You will truly be in control of the course of events that occur during your day. As a result, you will automatically become more productive, completing more "high yield" tasks sooner.

If you are spending all your time on the urgent tasks and the easy tasks, you'll never find the time to get done what's most important. At the end of the day, you will be drained of energy and find that you have accomplished very little. When you prioritize your time and your actions, you will get more results from your nine hundred-minute allotment for the day.

CREATING A TEAM

Once your nine hundred minutes are filled with productive activities, the only way to increase your output, or reduce the time it takes to accomplish your goals, is through the contributions of other people, through building a team of talented people around you. For example, I know very little about marketing on the internet or about managing a website. I have a website (www.jimbritt.com), but I was receiving very little from the site. When the website was first created, I learned about search engines and I paid to get the website positioned in order to drive more traffic to it, hopefully resulting in more sales. But none of the services ever worked, because the website wasn't configured properly to be search-engine friendly. Once I realized this, I partnered with someone who had the marketing expertise that I was missing.

When you team up with others in this way, it can give you a lot of leverage. It will free up your mind and time so that you can invest in what you are best at doing, allowing you to get more done in less time. And it can help you expand the scope and size of your business, not to mention increase your earning capacity. When you combine your talents with those of others, the combined knowledge and production output can be far greater than the sum of the separate contributions.

There are several things to keep in mind when building your team. First, make sure each member of your team is placed in a position where they can maximize their talents. The worst thing you can do is to place a person into a position simply because you have a person available and a position to fill. Make sure the person has the talents to fill the position, otherwise it will do more harm than good.

Second, be sure that you have like-minded team members, that their intentions do not create a "counter intention." In other words, make sure that they are all riding the horse in the direction it's going. If you have ten people on your team and only one is going in the wrong direction, that one person can destroy the efforts of the whole team. It's like running a relay with one person running in the wrong direction—you would have very little chance of winning the race.

Finally, monitor your team. Here's a simple method to do so, and these five words will help you to remember it: plan, production, progress, problems, and paint pictures.

It all starts with the *plan*—Make sure that everyone understands and fully supports your plan. You want them to feel that they are an integral part of the plan, that they feel some sense of ownership.

Production—What happened today? What did each team member do today that moved your business or project closer to success?

Progress—What progress has each team member made since the last time you talked? If he or she was committed to do a certain task or accomplish a project, what progress has been made?

Problems—Problems can immobilize. Realize that if a team member is stuck because of some problem he or she is facing, that person is out of business, out of productive capacity, until it gets handled. Check with him or her often to find out if he or she needs assistance or clarifications in any area. Remember, a problem can bring production and creativity to a halt and create a negative attitude until it is resolved.

Paint pictures—Make sure that every team member has a clear vision and you re-clarify the vision for him or her often. Let each person know that he or she is a key part of the team and of the end result that is produced. Give recognition often for a job well done. Whenever you're with a team member, make sure that he or she feels more empowered after having been with you. Talk to each about his or her goals and dreams and how he or she can accomplish them by being a part of your team, and then show the person how to get there. Often, employers hesitate to fully empower team members for fear that, if they do, the employee might leave and start his or her own business. My philosophy is this—better to have an empowered employee that may eventually leave than to have one who feels disempowered that you'll eventually have to fire.

If a team member starts to show signs of being a non-team player, you may find it necessary to have a talk with the person about his or her performance. And, if that doesn't work, you may have to replace him or her. There is nothing worse than to have someone on the team who is no longer a team player. The counter intention from just one team member gone bad can and will infect the rest of the team and their performance. A good rule of thumb that I apply is, "Don't give major time to people who have minor intention." If a team member is not performing and you don't see improvement after having a talk with him or her, end the relationship quickly and move on. This may sound cold, but you have to do what's best for the team and the business if you want it to be a success.

Get your team members working together for a common objective and show them what the accomplishment of that objective will mean to them individually. When my son Warren was eleven years old, we had several almond trees on our property. One day, as I was leaving for a trip, he asked me if I liked almonds and I said that I did. He was carrying a small box about eight inches in diameter. He said, "If I pick you a box of almonds, what would you pay me for them?" (He's very entrepreneurial.) I replied, "Two bucks." He said "Okay" and I left, never giving it another thought.

When I returned from my trip a few days later, Warren met me in the driveway and told me that I owed him thirty-two dollars. Stacked in the garage were sixteen boxes of almonds that he had picked for me. I guess I had failed to clarify just how many boxes I would pay for.

I said, "Warren, how did you pick all those almonds?" He said, "Well, I wanted the money to buy an electronic game from a friend for fifteen dollars. I told him that if he would help me pick the almonds, I would buy his game, and he agreed. My friend's brother also owned half interest in the game, so we got him to help as well."

I was amazed by the story and the coordinated team effort set in motion by an eleven-year-old, but it didn't end there. I then asked how he got the almonds out of the trees. He said, "Well, they were way up in the trees and we didn't know if we could get up there and knock them down. Bill (our neighbor across the street) was walking by and I asked him if he liked almonds. He said that he did, so I told him that if he would climb up in the trees and knock down the almonds, I would give him a box or two to take home. And that's the way we got them down."

Warren built a team with benefits for each member. "I like almonds"—that was a benefit for me. Warren's friend and the friend's brother wanted to sell the game, so they benefited from being on the team. And Bill became a team member because he liked almonds and saw a benefit for himself. I funded the whole project, and for that I got sixteen boxes of almonds and a story to tell! Warren had the vision of owning that game and a clear intention to have it. He then worked out the plan of action to make it happen, and everybody on the team came out a winner.

You may not need a team at this point in your business, but it's important to have the awareness that developing a team may be critical in the future in order to move to the next stage in your business development. Remember, you don't get very high sitting on the teeter-totter by yourself. So, are you going to spend your nine hundred minutes trying to accomplish something all by yourself or are you going to leverage your time and develop a team of like-minded individuals working together for a common goal?

Time doesn't care one way or the other—its only job is to count down the minutes, and it will do its job no matter what you do. You have a choice, though. You can be a victim of the passing of time or you can invest in it and reap huge rewards. Time is like a shopping spree: Look for ways during your day to shop with your time. The question is "What do you want to buy? And how much of your time do you want to invest for that purchase?"

DECIDE WHAT YOU'RE WORTH

You have nine hundred minutes to invest each day from which you create your future. What is each minute worth to you? A dollar a minute yields nine hundred dollars a day! Is that too low a sum? How about five, ten or even one hundred dollars a minute? Decide what your time is worth to you and how much of your nine hundred minutes each day you are willing to invest in a given project.

I calculate time when I'm conducting a seminar into the length of the program and the number of people attending. An athlete may calculate it into points made, a doctor into patient visits, a pool service into the number of pools he might clean in a day, a salesperson into units sold, and so on. Why not invest your time into a wonderful, profitable day, every day? When you value every moment, your day becomes priceless. By identifying what is most valuable to you, you know where to spend your time—by yourself, with friends or family, working on your business or career—it's up to you.

Remember, when a minute passes you by, it's gone forever, so act now! Nothing gets done without getting started. Nothing will happen if you live your life on hold, except time *ruthlessly* passing you by. In the end, will you look back and realize that you have only lived 10 percent of what you could have because of how you spent your time or the value you placed on it? Or will you have realized your dreams and all the adventures you promised yourself would happen? Will you have the financial freedom you want, or not? Will you have made a difference for others? Will you be happy and fulfilled in every way?

Your dreams are waiting for you, wanting you to act now. If not now, when? Only you have the time to turn your dreams into reality. In this present moment, you either act or you don't. Your dreams will be realized or they won't. You either move forward accomplishing your goals or time passes you by. Remember, it's not what you know that makes a difference, it's what you do with what you know that counts, and when you act more often, you get more results sooner.

5

Step Out of Your Comfort Zone

Most of us do the best we can with what we know, but some of us continue with our old ways knowing that there *could be* a better way. Why do we do it? It's because we're comfortable with our old ways—it's what we know, our comfort zone. And changing what we do, going against what we know or what got us where we are, would mean taking a risk. It would require stepping out of our comfort zone to do something that we haven't done before. The truth is that there is no other way to further develop ourselves.

Breaking out of your comfort zone involves risk and can bring up your deepest fears. "What if my business doesn't work?" "What if I lose my money?" "What if this opportunity isn't even real?" "What if I can't do it?" "What will others think of me being in this type of business?" Breaking out of your comfort zone can bring up the fear of failure. But so what if you fail? The greatest failure is not trying, staying where you are and letting fear run your life. Breaking out of your comfort zone can even bring fear of success. "If I'm successful, I may have to leave some of my friends behind. I may have to learn new skills or take on more responsibility."

Anything you want is just inches in front of your nose. It lies just outside your comfort zone, just one step away. If you want something different, you must ignore the conventional approach.

Be bold, and get ruthless with yourself about trying something different. Ordinarily, we achieve reasonable results because we take the reasonable approach. We look for ways to make modest improvements as we go, for small incremental gains that are comfortable. If you want to take giant steps forward, you must abandon normal thinking. Instead of trying once again—doing what you've always done with a little more intensity—try something totally different. To take a quantum leap forward requires an abrupt change in the way you do things.

DO SOMETHING IN A DIFFERENT WAY

About a year after I had opened one of my nutritional clinics, the advertisement that had once worked started to decline in effectiveness, so I decided to try something a bit different. Instead of running the ad in the conventional way, I turned it upside down. The reader had to make a conscious effort to turn the paper upside down to read the ad. It worked! In fact, for the next few months, it worked better than it had when it first started to run in the conventional way.

What I'm saying is this: try being illogical instead of logical, try being a little bold. If you want to get in a house and the front door is locked, does that mean you can't get in? No, it means that the conventional way is not an option. So, you try the back door. If that doesn't work, try a window or the chimney. If there's a wall in front of you, first look for the gate and walk through. Don't climb the wall unless you have to. But if you have to, then do it. Think up and do something new!

Our natural tendency when we meet with resistance is to return to safety, to the basics, to what we know or do best. But doing what you do best could be the worst thing possible, especially if it is getting you nowhere. For example, let's say that you are in sales and are really good at closing the sale. What if you became really good at making a more effective presentation? Wouldn't that produce a better result faster? I mean, you have to make the presentation anyway, so why not get so good at making the presentation that you don't have to close? It saves you one step and, more importantly, it saves you time.

Having faith in the familiar can be a trap, and you trigger the trap when you invest your time and effort in what "should" work simply because it worked before. What worked before may or may not work again. If you want to get ahead faster, you have to break out of the rut you've created. Following your rut is an addictive behavior—you must create new patterns. If what you are doing no longer works, don't do it anymore! And if you simply quit doing what's not working, you'll discover new possibilities. When you focus on trying harder to do what's not working, there's no space left for anything new to come forth.

Giant leaps forward come when you seek a faster, simpler, and more efficient solution. Overall, you will expend much less energy and waste much less time. Look for a way to do more with less. Business and financial growth is an ongoing process. Every step you take leads to the next, and there are many steps on your way toward financial success. But there are ways right in front of your nose to bypass many of the normal steps. They may be uncomfortable, but it will be well worth the discomfort.

Making a quantum leap in your level of success will demand a willingness to make mistakes and to feel uncomfortable at times. You cannot hide in a safe zone of behavior where you have beaten or avoided the odds of failing. An unwillingness to encounter defeat, to run into problems, or to face discomfort will not move you forward. In fact, that is the one thing beyond all others that will keep you stuck where you are right now. Unless you allow yourself to make mistakes, to fail, you will never have the opportunity to test the limits of what you truly are capable of accomplishing.

If you're experiencing no difficulties or discomfort, you have probably aimed too low. Breaking out of your comfort zone and moving to the next level of success is destabilizing, and what you want to do is to deliberately destabilize yourself to break out of old habit patterns that represent your status quo. Doing something in a different way can feel risky and even threatening. What you have to do is to look at the hidden risk of staying where you are or repeating behaviors that do not work. Ask yourself, "What am I risking if I *don't* step out of my comfort zone and do it differently?" The risk is that if you keep doing it the same way, nothing will ever change.

Risk is inevitable. It's not something you can decide to live without—unless of course you want to stay where you are. Something is always at stake and your job is to decide which risks to take. So, choose carefully. And don't kid yourself that playing it safe is the best way to beat the odds of failing—it also beats the odds of succeeding. You will never achieve real success by playing it safe. Playing it safe is the surest way to stay where you are, and that's the biggest risk in my opinion.

TAKE A FULL-SPECTRUM VIEW

Moving forward means that you have to go beyond the zone of the familiar, beyond the comfortable, but it doesn't mean being reckless. Taking that giant leap forward doesn't mean gambling or risking everything you have. It simply means that you take advantage of opportunity instead of ignoring it and that you let go of the excuses you have always used for not taking action.

Frame the opportunity and take a full-spectrum view, looking at it from different angles and then taking appropriate action. For example, if an opportunity required money and you had none, look at the opportunity as if you actually had the money. Then, if the opportunity looks real and profitable, consider how you could raise the money. There is always more than one way to get the job done.

Being open to risk and willing to take a full-spectrum view will unmask the truth, revealing the only thing that may be standing in your way. And once you know the truth of the situation, you can choose to take action or not. You must risk believing in yourself and the decisions you make. Risk making the assumption that you can become financially successful to whatever level you choose.

Otherwise, you risk settling for only a small fraction of what life could provide for you. I'm not talking about taking a big chance, but rather giving yourself a chance.

The solution is not to challenge the odds of success but rather to challenge your limiting beliefs. Until you challenge your beliefs of what you think you can achieve, you'll never know how far you can go. Remember, a belief is something that you have decided is true, but the reality is that it may not be true at all. Learn to suspend your beliefs and look for the real truth. Instead of believing that something will or will not work, look for evidence proving beyond any doubt that it can or it cannot work. And if you decide that it can work, act as if your success is absolutely guaranteed.

I know that making that giant leap forward is a foreign idea because most of us are not trained to think that way. It's like a doctor. Most doctors are trained to treat the symptom, not the cause, of the problem. Those doctors who take the giant leap forward and actually begin treating the cause of a disease, instead of just treating the symptom, will end up in the forefront of the thriving wellness trend. Having no money is simply a symptom, and focusing on that symptom will not make you more money, just like focusing on treating the disease symptom won't heal the body.

It is said that a human being only utilizes about 10 percent of his or her brain. What that means to me is that humans are in a resourceful, productive state only 10 percent of the time. The rest of the time they are lost in nonproductive belief systems and old habit patterns. What if you could double your effectiveness to 20 percent, what would that do for your productivity? What if you could be more productive just 20 percent of the time? How about 30 percent or 50 percent—what would happen?

My point is that everyone has the potential to do much more than what they are currently doing. It may be that you're skeptical because you've never done more than 10 percent before. You only have the factual data about yourself, based on past history. Doubting yourself that way is called "mind chatter" and it can ruin your chances at success if you let it. If you buy into the mind chatter, your thinking will be flawed. At some point in most people's lives, they simply accepted flawed thinking as "correct" thinking. The question is, how do you know if your thinking is flawed or if it is correct? You challenge it: Who taught you to think that way? What if they didn't know the truth? What if the person who taught them didn't know? How did it really work for them?

As a child, you took bold steps and big risks, and you challenged yourself. You had faith that you could do it, didn't you? Now is the time to dig deep inside to rediscover that faith. It's time to put those inhibiting beliefs to rest and go for it with everything you've got. For now, just suspend your beliefs. I don't want you to believe me—just give it a go and see what happens. You don't even have to be convinced that you will succeed in a big way. All I ask is that you don't keep hanging on to limiting beliefs about your personal limits. Just start to act as if you have complete faith—do what you would do if you knew you were going to succeed. Have complete conviction.

Doubt is the biggest problem and does the most damage. It creates uncertainty, uncertainty creates lack of clarity, and lack of clarity immobilizes. So, don't give doubt any mental space. Move forward boldly as if it was absolutely incomprehensible that you would experience anything other than success.

FAILING DOESN'T MEAN YOU'RE A FAILURE

To achieve more in less time, you have to create some inner chaos for yourself. That's the only way you know you're truly making progress that will last. Be prepared for the possibility of confusion, anxiety, and failings along the way as part of opening yourself up to new methods that have the potential to deliver maximum performance gains. When stepping out into something new like starting a business, problems are just part of the process. In fact, problems are the reason you are going into business, not proof that your ambitions are futile or that you should give up. Businesses solve problems. That's the nature of business. Problems create opportunities, and taking advantage of the opportunity by solving the problem is how people get rich. The bigger the problem you solve, the more the potential earnings.

Everything looks like a failure when you're in the middle of it. It doesn't matter if you're writing a book, building a new business from the start, or baking a cake. You can't bake a cake without getting the kitchen messy, can you? If you blast a rocket toward the moon, about ninety percent of the time it is off course and you are spending most of the time correcting the problem. You could say that it "fails" its way to the moon by making mistakes and correcting them.

If you are off course going to the moon and miss it, that's a big mistake! If you want to make any mission a success, you don't turn back when you're a little off course—you correct. When you start to feel uncomfortable and a little outside of your comfort zone, it's easy to turn on yourself and sink back into your old ways. You may avoid the pain, but remember the old adage, "No pain, no gain!"

This is a critical part of making progress. Don't give up! Discomfort and obstacles belong in your way—overcoming them is a sign of progress. Avoiding the discomfort and pain can make you retreat toward the "safety" of the old you, the trap of the familiar. Discomfort does not mean defeat, unless you are unwilling to move past it and to actually deal with the pain of change. So, go looking for discomfort, for a problem to solve, and use it as a stepping stone to move forward. Don't interpret an obstacle, discomfort, pain, or failure as proof that you should quit—take them as evidence of your progress toward your desired results. Discomfort is a resource to help you find the edge of your current capacities, but also realize that your current capacities do not represent your full potential.

PREPARE FOR A WILD RIDE

Prepare yourself for a potentially wild ride as an entrepreneur. You're going to cover unfamiliar terrain and encounter obstacles you've never faced before. At times, you may feel like the safety chain that links you with your past behavior patterns is being stretched to the limit. And when your normal reaction is to hold on tightly to your old ways in order to avoid the pain, you have to learn to let go and move on. If you want success, the only way to have it is to stay focused on where you want to go, continue the pursuit despite the obstacles, and learn from your mistakes. You will be giving up a large degree of safety and security and may even have to contend with people who were part of your support system in the past who no longer support you in your endeavor.

The only risks that aren't a little scary are the ones you've already outgrown. If you aren't feeling some discomfort, the risk you're taking probably isn't worthy of you. A high comfort level provides you with solid evidence that you're "playing it safe" and not really testing your limits at all. If you do the one thing that you fear most, the death of that fear is certain. Courage is the antidote to fear, so press on.

You may hear the word *impossible* coming from other people or from your own mind chatter. *Impossible* is just a word that is tossed around by small-thinking people who find it easier to live within the circumstances they've been handed rather than explore the power they have to change their circumstances. "Impossible" is just someone's opinion, and opinions are like belly buttons—everybody has one. Look at "impossible" as a challenge, as potential waiting to be uncovered. If you think something is impossible, guess what—it is! Start to view *impossible* as nothing more than a word created to help you move past your comfort zone.

6

Overcome Self-Imposed Limitations

Here's a story about a very successful entrepreneur and business person. One morning, he was taking a leisurely drive along a deserted country road when suddenly his attention was drawn toward some activity out in the middle of a field under a tree. As he got closer, he saw that it was a farmer running around and around under a huge apple tree chasing about 200 little pigs. Curious, he decided to stop and observe for a while. He noticed that when the farmer finally caught a pig, he would hold it up and let it eat an apple off the tree. The farmer would then put down the pig and begin chasing another. Again, as he caught it, he would hold it up to the tree, and let it eat an apple. He continued the same process over and over for more than an hour.

Finally, the man, being entrepreneurial minded, thought to himself, "There must be a better, more efficient way." So, he walked out into the field to have a chat with the farmer. As he approached the farmer, he said, "Excuse me, I've been watching you for about an hour now. Would you mind telling me what you are doing?"

The farmer responded, "Well, I'm feeding these apples to my pigs. They like apples."

Perplexed, the man said, "Why don't you just pick all the apples off the tree, throw them on the ground, and let the pigs run around and eat the apples? Wouldn't that save a lot of time?"

And the farmer, with a puzzled look on his face, responded, "What's time to a pig?"

What do you think is the moral to this story? And what does it have to do with building a successful business or becoming financially free? Do you think there might be a better way for the farmer to feed apples to his pigs? You might say, "Of course!" But that's from your perspective. How about from the farmer's perspective? Probably not, otherwise he would be using it, wouldn't he?

In order to attain a different result, you have to *do* something differently. And in order to do something differently, you must first *know* something different to do. Perhaps the farmer just didn't think anything different could be done, which brings up my next point—in order to know something different, you must first suspect that your present method of operation or understanding needs improving. You must first become aware that you *need* to do something in a different way before you *can* do something in a different way.

It is impossible to achieve the next level of success with the same thinking, beliefs, and behaviors that got you where you are today. In order to make new advancements, you must develop new, more productive ways of acting. There is no system that I or anyone else could offer to change a person's perceptions unless he or she thought his or her perceptions needed changing and was open to a new and better method. I may offer ideas, but each individual must take the initiative and observe his or her own methods, behaviors, and beliefs, and make the choice to change his or her own ways. If I believe that my way is the only way, then I will be heavily invested in protecting my belief. But if I remain open to learning better, more efficient methods—if something or someone wakes me up to the truth and I discover that I have a choice—I am then free to look with a new perspective.

LEARNING TO SUSPEND ALL BELIEFS

Limiting beliefs are specific things you think about yourself that cause you to conclude, "I'm not worthy of success." Those beliefs influence you, your thinking, your behavior, and your success. So, the first person you have to convince of your value is you! Often you live with a limiting belief about yourself until you become numb and no longer notice it. That's what I call living in a comfort zone, and in this context, "comfort" really means lazy, stagnant, or satisfied with the status quo. It means that you have chosen to "play it safe" because the fear associated with going for more is a risk that your limiting belief won't let you take.

If you find yourself in this situation, ask yourself what it is you are avoiding. You may discover that you have a fear of failing or you may fear the very success that you say you want. You've no doubt heard the saying, "What goes up must come down." You may be thinking that if you succeed even one time, that everyone will expect you to keep it up. Or that you will not only have to do it again, but you should do it better each time. You may view being successful as a lot of pressure, so your limiting belief tells you to not take the risk. I don't believe in being reckless, but I do believe in requiring more of myself. If you want advancement faster, you must start immediately to program yourself for success by setting clear objectives that involve stretching yourself, growing, and utilizing more of your skills (or developing new ones).

Our beliefs are what hold us back or what move us forward. For example, you may be broke right now, therefore you say, "I am broke." Or you may possess a degree in psychology, and therefore you say, "I am a psychologist." You may say, "I resent successful people," therefore "I am resentful of success." These are all beliefs that we have developed about ourselves that restrict our productivity. And if we are not careful, these beliefs will become the identity upon which all our decisions are based. Your belief is something that *you* have decided is true, when in fact it may not be true at all—it is simply your opinion.

Our beliefs become so imprinted on our self-identity that we build powerful support systems to reassure one another that what we do, what we have, and what we believe in is who we really are. Rather than change ourselves, we want to change outside circumstances, change other people, change the government, change our relationship or our job, and so on, in an attempt to change our lives. You might think, "I hate my job and if I could just get another job, then things would be different." The only thing that would be different is that you would have another job you hate. You have to change yourself and your beliefs if you want to change your circumstances.

Some people believe that if they have a good enough reason for not succeeding, they can avoid taking risks and breaking out of their comfort zone. They use a smokescreen of excuses designed to distract themselves from the real truth or to avoid the pain of change. Some people use being in a state of emotional upheaval as an excuse. "If I'm upset, you can't expect me to be responsible for my results." Being the victim is a common reason used to explain away a lack of results. But victimhood is simply a belief—a belief that can be changed.

GOING BEYOND BELIEVING

Going beyond belief and seeing the truth behind your beliefs is where success starts. Knowing the real reasons for not succeeding previously will help you adjust your actions and produce the results you want. Those who learn to see the truth behind their actions and to know reality, and those who are willing to let go of old habits and take full responsibility for their actions, are in the best position to experience success in their lives.

The past is what holds you back in the present. I'm not saying you must forget the past, but reminding yourself that the past is over is a good place to start. The past is not the present and the past has no basis for reality in the present. The results you did or didn't produce yesterday do not count today. Whether your past was filled with success and victory or failure and loss, it doesn't matter. You can start anew today! The present is not the past either. Today is simply today, and only through your actions today will you achieve success, or not.

In order to change your feeling or belief about a current condition, you don't need to analyze it to death. That is like trying to deflect an avalanche by knowing which snowflake was the first to start tumbling down the mountainside. In an avalanche, it's what is happening here and now that counts, isn't it? The only thing you need to know is how to get out from under it!

And in your business, whatever it may be, it's what you're doing here and now that counts, the only thing that can count. The real road block is your old set of beliefs, especially if you don't realize you have them.

I'm not talking about self-improvement, positive thinking, or motivation. In my opinion, self-improvement is self-addition, positive thinking is covering up the truth with frills and glitter, and motivation is suppressing or ignoring reality. All three give a false sense of self by replacing reality with where we wish we were. If those things could have worked to produce success, everyone would be a success by now, don't you think? We've all had enough positive thinking and motivation to last a lifetime!

I'm talking about "self-correction," "correct thinking," and "correct action." If you truly desire success, what you need is self-correction through correct thinking backed up by correct action. The self-correction method of change can be carried out by you; it does not require a therapist or someone showing up to motivate you. You don't need that at all and no one could do it for you anyway. A therapist won't find anything that you can't find or don't already know. Only *you* can change you.

Think of it as re-creating or re-inventing yourself. If you don't like who you are or where you are in life, change it and do something differently. Reinventing yourself is a basic principle at work at every moment of your life. It's behind the creation of your personality, your mind-set, your business, your success, your health, your relationships, and everything else in your life. Every time you act, whether positive or negative, you add strength to the motive that's behind what you've done.

Let's say, for example, that you find yourself in a financial slump. If you continue to think you are in a slump and remain there long enough, you could develop the attitude or belief that you are not worthy of making money in the first place. And every time you act upon that thought, "I'm not worthy of making money," the underlying belief behind it is intensified and strengthened.

This pertains to any idea—about money, about yourself, about others, about success, about your abilities, about the world. Whatever the belief, it is intensified when you focus on it or act upon it, because each act retypes the message in your mind. It strengthens your dendrites, the branching processes that conduct nerve impulses in neurons, a crucial component in building your memories. You could consider success and failure a "battle of the dendrites." You have to win the war against old beliefs, against the negative dendrites, in order to experience something new. There's no room for both on the playing field.

Here's the key to winning the battle: When the message you receive—such as "I don't deserve success"—is *not* acted upon, it becomes weaker, like a fadeout in a movie. When the message is acted upon, it becomes clearer and brighter, prompting more of the same and strengthening the dendrites. The most important factor is learning to recognize the truth behind your actions, so that you understand and see the connection between the motive, the act, and the result. Once you know the truth, you can then decide to let go of your old beliefs. You can let them wither away from lack of attention.

It's much like having a disease and not knowing the cure—what you might call "disease paranoia." The person with the disease is always worried and thinks there's a conspiracy against him. He senses certain weaknesses in himself and thinks that everyone knows them. He thinks that everyone is out to see him fail. But don't worry, everyone else is too busy with their own paranoia to notice yours anyway. So, where does this paranoia come from? If you have that paranoia, failure syndrome, money block—whatever you want to call it—you gave it to yourself. And only you can take it away. Paranoia is the self-creation principle at work in a very observable form. We all have destructive habits and every time we indulge a bad habit, we strengthen it and give it a greater grip.

How do you stop this paranoia? By seeking out the action or habit that reinforces it, and then refraining from that action. You stop feeding it. You challenge the underlying belief by asking yourself, "What do I believe about success?" "How did I come to believe this?" "What if it's not true?" "Who taught me to believe this way?" "What if they were just acting out of their own paranoia?" "Is this belief real or something I created based on false information?" Let me save you some time—it's something you created. We all do it.

If you discover a nonproductive habit or belief, ask yourself if there's any reason to hang on to it. If not, let it go and move on. If you're doing something that's not working for you, then don't do it anymore. That's the simple solution! Instead, do something that will take you in the direction you want to go.

CHANGING A BELIEF

The first and the most important step in changing a belief is to observe yourself and admit that something needs to change. The second step is to have the intention to change, to develop a new, more productive belief. The third step is the willingness to take responsibility, to step out of your comfort zone and take a risk, to let go of the old ways and to do something in a different way. And, fourth, you have to commit to change in order to move past the old habit or belief. If you want to change, you have to be willing to look for the truth behind your actions and circumstances, and then you must take full responsibility for changing them. Once you see the truth, you can choose to act in ways that no longer reinforce the unwanted habit.

For example, perhaps you worry all the time about something you have no control over. What could you do instead of worry? How about doing nothing? And will doing nothing help ease the worry? Of course it will! Now, if there is something you could do about it, then let go of your worry and take action. Let's say you are faced with a difficult situation and you need to make a telephone call to confront the issue. Instead of putting it off and worrying about the outcome, which will waste countless "power points" of valuable time, let go of your worry and make the call. Just get it over with and move on. Worry and procrastination waste time and drain away energy.

Remember, what you give attention to will grow in strength. What you are worried about can become an even bigger problem if you do not deal with it quickly—at least in your own mind, which is where the problem was in the first place. On the other hand, if you're worried about something and there's no action you can take to resolve the problem, then let go of the worry and do nothing. Or do something else that is more productive. Either way, when you let go and take action or you simply let go, you weaken the habit. Defending or giving energy to your fear will only increase your fear and strengthen the problem.

When you take a chance and step out of your comfort zone and confront the issue, it's true that you might get hurt. But you'll find that it's much better than spending your whole life on guard, worrying about getting hurt or under a blanket in the corner hoping no one will notice you. That's even worse, in my opinion, than actually getting hurt. When you act with strength and courage, you will reinforce that premise—you'll become stronger and more courageous.

In America, we have the freedom to make our own choices. We can even choose to be rich or not. How about your personal freedom? Are you willing to stand up and fight for it? Are you willing to do whatever it takes to maintain it? Are you willing to choose to be rich?

OVERCOMING MONEY LIMITATIONS

A few years ago, researchers did a behavioral experiment involving fish in a fish tank. They let the fish swim freely for some time, then one day they put in a glass divider, cutting the size of the tank in half. Then, they placed all the fish in one end of the tank. At first, because the glass divider wasn't visible, the fish would bump their heads into the glass. After some time passed, the fish would stop just short of hitting their head. Then, a surprising thing took place: The researchers removed the divider, but the fish were so used to avoiding the pain of hitting their heads against the glass that they all stayed in one end of the tank, as if the glass partition was still in place.

I believe that most people have the same approach to making money—they are so used to hitting their heads against the wall that they settle for less in order to avoid the pain. The pain has caused them to become resistant to new ways of thinking and they become trapped by their own fear.

Learning how to use your mind to attract wealth is the first step. I have found that the more you struggle and the more effort you put forth, the less you actually achieve. Successful people know how their energy works and how their mind works. They have discovered how to focus the various forms of energy—time, creativity, physical vitality, thinking, and even money—into reality, and they do it with ease.

Spend some time discovering your relationship toward money. It may seem as you go through this exercise that you are going into uncharted territory. And if it seems that way, you probably need the experience. Your experience with money began when you were young and it has had a major influence on how you relate to money today. Think about it for a moment.

- When did you first hear about money?
- Who first told you about money? How did that person relate to money? Did you perceive them as rich or poor?
- What were your living conditions and emotional climate like at that time?
- When did you earn your first money?
- When and where did you first spend it?
- When did you first lose some money and how did that make you feel?

I'd like you to get a pen and paper and answer the above questions regarding your experience with money. Begin by writing the story of your life, using as your theme how you relate to money. Don't worry about proper grammar, spelling, or sentence structure. Write your story in narrative form, beginning with your earliest childhood memories about money and bringing your story to the present time. Let me give you some additional questions to trigger your thoughts.

- When you were a child, what do you remember most about money?
- What conversations did you hear from your parents about money? How would you describe their relationship with money?
- Were you given an allowance each week and did you have to work to get it? Did you appreciate it? Did you work hard for it?
- As a child, how would you describe your relationship toward money? How did it make you feel?
- How do you relate to people today who have more money than you? Do you feel relaxed around them or intimidated?
- If someone described your relationship with money from their point of view, how would they view you?
- Where do you see yourself financially five years from now?
- Financially, where did you see yourself today five years ago?
- How has your relationship with money changed in the last five years?
- What do you spend your money on? What do you hold back spending your money on?
- Have you dreamed in the past of someday having a certain amount of money? Is that a reality in your life today? What progress have you made?
- What is your relationship with money today? Do you see any

connection to your past relationship toward money? Are there any glaring issues or themes that keep popping up?

• Do you have any regrets in your past or present regarding money?

As you write your biography about your relationship with money, just remember that any painful past or present issues you discover point you in a direction where healing is needed. When you finish your story, give it a title and congratulate yourself on being willing to write it. Seeing your relationship with money is very important to the progression of your success. As you study the findings, you'll make important insights that will show you a whole new way to relate to money.

Think More Abundantly

Let me offer you some additional exercises that will help you reprogram your mind about money matters and show you how to have more in your life with less effort. Remember, it is much easier to have money in your life than it is to struggle to have it. If having enough money is a problem for you, you are the one who struggles to keep money away. All you have to do is stop the struggle and change your focus and what you believe about money.

The first step is to begin to show gratitude for any money that enters your life. Instead of complaining about how much you don't have, change your focus and be grateful for the multiple ways that you are already rich. Did you know that if you earn two thousand dollars each month, you are in the top 10 percent of income earners on earth? And even if you earn only two thousand dollars a year, you are wealthier than 85 percent of the people on the planet. When you begin to focus on what you have rather than what you don't have, you'll discover that you are already wealthy. Give thanks, and give it often!

Feel and act as if you are already rich. In other words, act as if what you want is already yours. That doesn't mean that you should quit your job, buy a private jet, and travel the world.

Rather, get in touch with the feeling of having what you want. What would it feel like to have all the money you ever wanted? How would you act? How would you spend your day? How would you conduct your business? Start to do some of the things you would do if you were rich: Stay in a better hotel when you travel, eat better meals and drink better wine, take a limo instead of a cab on occasion, use valet parking instead of parking your own car. What I'm suggesting is that you learn to take the course of action that you think you can't afford to take. Little by little, start to live in your dream fulfilled, learn to "be there now" in your mind and heart. When you do, with each little thing, begin to notice how it feels inside to be wealthy. You will be absolutely amazed at how the universe will provide more of what you feel inside.

Try this. The next time you are about to buy something—a nice meal in a restaurant, for example—go for the one you want instead of considering the price. Order the thirty-dollar meal instead of the one that costs twenty-two dollars. Better yet, on occasion, order without looking at the price of the meal. If you are buying clothing, go for something that is just a little higher quality even though it costs a little more. Instead of giving the parking attendant two dollars to park your car, give him five dollars. You will be amazed by two things: One is how much better you feel, and the other is how much better your service will be the next time.

Even though these are just tiny steps, what you are doing is teaching your mind to think more abundantly. You are beginning to expand what you previously thought were your limitations. And the more you do it, the more the universe will provide for you to do more of the same. A dollar bill is printed on the same paper as a hundred dollar bill, there are just two more zeros on it. Start to think in hundreds instead of ones, or better yet, in millions instead of thousands.

In order to attract wealth, you have to open your mind to new ways of thinking and acting. Be open to the new ways in which money will flow to you. The amount of money doesn't matter—begin to notice how even small, unexpected amounts flow to you.

Your subconscious mind, or the universe, or whatever you want to call it, doesn't distinguish between ten dollars and ten thousand dollars. All it knows is how you feel and it will provide you with more of the same.

Which would make you feel more abundant, having five hundred dollars in your pocket or having that same amount in the bank? I got into the habit of carrying five hundred dollars in my pocket over thirty years ago and still do it today, even though I pay for almost everything with a credit card. It just feels right to me. Besides, as a friend of mine says, "What if you see a Girl Scout selling cookies and you have no cash?"

It also works in many other ways as well. If you feel guilty, for example, for charging someone for work you've done or taking money for a product you've sold them, or you charge them less because you feel guilty, you are supporting a belief in lack and setting yourself up to attract more of the same. Be open to attracting and accepting money into your life. Do not feel guilty about accepting money, instead feel gratitude when you receive it.

Begin to think of money like breathing. Focus on your breath for a moment. Notice how your breath flows naturally—it flows in and it flows out without effort. Now, think of money as you focus on your breath, flowing in, flowing out, flowing in, flowing out. Think of money as energy, flowing in, flowing out. Money comes and money goes, there's always enough, flowing in, flowing out. Begin to look at money in this way.

FINDING MONEYMAKING OPPORTUNITIES

Learn to be open to moneymaking opportunities. They are everywhere. All you have to do is be open to taking advantage of them. Stop for a moment and look around you. How many things can you see that someone has made millions of dollars on? The very seat you are sitting in probably made someone millions. The car you drive, the house you live in, the shopping mall where you shop were created by people who had an idea and took action. Look into your past—are there opportunities you wish you had not missed? Everybody has a few. How many more do you think you missed simply because you weren't open to seeing or receiving them? It could be career opportunities that passed you by, investment opportunities, personal opportunities, and on and on. The difference between rich people and average income earners is that rich people realize that opportunities are all around, and they are always on the lookout and ready to take advantage of the right ones. Keep an open mind and be ready.

Some believe that the rich are simply lucky. Well, they are—lucky that they were open to opportunities and lucky that they took advantage of the right one at the right time. You also can be blessed with incredible luck if you apply the same philosophy as the rich. If you enter the same office building every day, it's likely that there's someone there that may hold the key to your opportunity, someone you'd love to meet. Every morning, you see him or her get into the elevator and go up to his or her office, and every evening you see him or her come down. And every time you see him or her, you wish that you could meet him or her. There are two things you might want to consider: first, realize that wishes are for poor people, and second, *get on the elevator!* That's how successful people get lucky—they get on the elevator, they create their own luck. Success is something you attract by your philosophy. Great opportunities are reserved for searchers, not wishers. They are reserved for the lucky few, and winners learn to develop a performance philosophy.

Take a moment and do a little exercise: Write down all the moneymaking opportunities that you could take advantage of right now. Don't think about the investment, your experience, or anything else that might limit your possibilities. Let your mind wander. You could purchase a franchise, start a landscaping company or a pool cleaning service, invest in real estate rental properties, join a network marketing company, manufacture a new gadget, and so on. These are just some ideas to get you going. Start writing and don't stop until you have at least twenty opportunities. I'll bet you'll find plenty of ideas just waiting for you to take advantage of them, and there will always be opportunities for those open to receiving them. All the ones you list may not be ideal for you, but if you keep an open mind, you'll eventually find the one that "lights your wick!"

If you want a different result, you have to break free of the backward thinking that plagues most of society. The rest of the world thinks that America is a culture that is blessed with money and opportunity. They also think that we are obsessed with money. We are, in fact, a culture obsessed by the fear of money, whether it is about having it or not having it. Most people think backwards about money because they don't have enough. And they will never have more until they do something in a different way and start to look at money in a different way. When you begin to change how you look at money, you become in "magnetic harmony" with money, attracting more of it into your life. The opposite is also true, so you want to avoid people who are poverty-minded, who bring down your energy level and make you feel and think small.

TAKE A RICH PERSON TO DINNER

Here's an interesting exercise: Take a rich person out to dinner and pick up the tab! Take him or her for a seven-course gourmet dinner, buy a bottle of wine, dessert, and an after-dinner drink. Keep the person at dinner as long as possible, and during that time ask questions. Ask him or her how he or she made the money, how he or she got started, how hard it was, and ask about the person's beliefs about money. Ask and listen carefully to what he or she says!

You may have the attitude that the rich person should buy the dinner. After all, he or she can afford it, right? But the rich person doesn't need the education, you do. And the price of a meal is a low cost for an education. The greatest cost is missing out because you don't see the value in it.

Become aware of how you relate to money and success. Avoid feeling fearful and anxious about money and success. The more aware you become, the easier it will be to change your perception. Begin to do everything with great enthusiasm—put everything you've got into what you do. If you are going to watch a sunset, take it to the next level and listen to it and feel it. That feeling will bring more abundance into your life. Why? Because things that make you feel good attract more things into your life that make you feel good.

Don't worry that you don't have the talent, that you are too young or too old. Don't worry that you don't have the money, the right contacts, or enough experience. Don't worry about anything because there is no intelligence in worry. There is absolutely nothing needed to bring more abundance into your life than what is already inside you waiting to be exposed. You have all you need. You have the gift—all you have to do is to unwrap it. The real gift is your imagination and how you feel. You can feel, think, and imagine in any way you choose.

CHANGING HABIT PATTERNS

In order to be successful in most businesses, you have to sell yourself first. If the customer or client doesn't buy *you*, then they won't buy your product or service. We all have habits that may not be serving our best interests. All habits, good or bad, are self-imposed, and the bad ones can be changed. To help you to recognize habits that may cripple your chance of success, here are some specific things you may want to consider.

The habit doesn't accomplish anything. It only costs you time, energy, and money. Perhaps you have a habit of making personal calls during the time you have designated to make business calls or doing non-business activities during the time you are supposed to be working at your business. With closer observation, you may discover that this habit is fueled by a fear of being rejected by someone when you make a business call or a fear that your business may not succeed. So, you use personal calls as a way of justifying to yourself that you are busy making calls or doing business activities. This sort of "busyness" versus business could lead to your business not being successful. What you are really doing is hiding from the truth, and if you want success, you must look for the truth, not hide from it. Then, you must take action that leads you toward what you want instead of away from it.

The habit is physically harmful. Smoking, drinking too much, and overeating are obvious examples of this type of problem. These habits can cause stress, cloud your thinking, and make you less productive overall, not to mention that they may shorten your life span. If you have any of these habits, my suggestion is to stop. Seek professional help if you need to. The discipline needed to break these harmful habits is the same discipline you will need to be successful in business anyway. Both require a firm decision-making process. If you want to be a success in business, you have to first make a decision to be a success, and the same holds true when breaking a destructive habit.

The habit irritates others. Maybe you have the habit of always asking for compliments or standing right in someone's face when you speak. Perhaps you clear your throat before each sentence. Maybe you tap your finger on the table or constantly insert words like "you know" or "okay" into your sentences. Observe yourself. When do you practice your irritating habit? Notice what you're feeling at the time and you may discover that a need for acceptance or a fear of rejection leads to your actions.

Many years ago, when I first began my speaking career, a woman came up to me after one of my seminars and said, "You had some great things to say, but I was distracted by the number of times you said 'okay' during your talk." When I denied it, she said, "I taped your talk and you might want to listen to it." I kept her tape on my desk for about a month before I worked up the courage to listen to it. What an eye opener! I discovered that with each statement I made, I would end with "okay." I realized that I was seeking approval from my audience. I made a decision to never use "okay" again while addressing a group. I never knew I had the habit until I stopped to observe myself, thanks to the woman who taped my program. So, whatever the habit, if it's irritating to others, you can bet it is costing you business.

The habit makes you look foolish. This doesn't mean you have to break every habit that someone else doesn't like, but you might want to take a realistic look and ask yourself what habits you have that may be costing you credibility, and therefore costing you business. For example, I know someone who promotes a health product, and she smokes. She does very well in her business, but my question is, "How much better could she be doing if she got rid of a habit that causes her to lose credibility?"

I knew a fellow who always wore a tie that was about six inches too short and the back part of his tie was longer than the front. Perhaps I shouldn't have let it bother me, but I knew it was costing him business, and since he worked for me, I knew it was costing the company, too. Everyone in the office talked about it. One day, I simply told him how it looked and what others were saying. As it turned out, he just didn't know how to tie a tie. I taught him in about five minutes and both our problems were solved. He thanked me for having the courage to tell him and I felt better having done so—not to mention he looked much better.

You don't approve of your own habit. It violates your own credibility, values, or integrity in some way. Maybe you overstate or exaggerate your product in order to entice someone to buy. You know you shouldn't, but you do it anyway. Perhaps you tell others things that were told to you in confidence. No one knows except you, and it bothers you, but you do it anyway. Engage in a little self-reflection to discover why you do it. Maybe it's for recognition, to make it look like you know something that others don't. If you become more self-observant, you can better see how you come across to others. You may be hurting your credibility without even knowing it.

You get three huge payoffs for breaking bad habits: You get rid of something you didn't want or need in the first place; you develop new insights into how you affect others; and it greatly improves your chances of being successful. I wish that you could break unwanted habits without using any willpower, but you can't. You basically have to go "cold turkey"—just quit. Begin by making a fundamental choice not to have the habit, to be something else.

MAKE A FUNDAMENTAL CHOICE

Let's say you want to quit smoking because it's affecting your health as well as your business. It will do you absolutely no good to try to taper off. When you taper off smoking, you still see yourself as a smoker—you can't be a smoker and a nonsmoker at the same time. The first thing you must do if you want to quit is to make a fundamental choice to *be* a nonsmoker. Not *try* to quit, but to *become* a nonsmoker. You have to make a decision to honor your own health more than the habit. The rest is easier once you achieve the mind-set to see yourself as a nonsmoker.

Your success in business is the same—you have to make a fundamental choice to *be* a success. You have to honor your success more than you do failure or your present condition or your habit. Once you've made that choice and developed the success mindset, the rest is easy. Success comes easily if you leave no room for failure. Observe your habits as they relate to your business and to your life, because they both interact. Do you say "yes" when you want to say "no?" Begin to notice what seems to bring out certain habits. Is it certain people's actions or specific situations that make you feel uncertain? The more you know about your nonproductive habits, the more you will be prepared to break them once and for all.

There are all kinds of habits, some good and some not so good. One thing they all have in common is that they are voluntary and artificial, created and controlled by you. You create the *bad* and the *good,* and you can live without the bad ones. All it takes to change them is a decision to do so, backed up by discipline. Most of us have habits that we don't like and would like to get rid of, habits that we've been meaning to break "one of these days." If you want success faster, now is the time. Breaking a bad habit has its own reward: It will improve your business, your success, your life, and your personal growth overall.

Intention is the starting point for change. In order to make a permanent change, you must first have the intention to understand yourself. Self-knowledge is the beginning step toward success. It cannot be given to you by learning a system or from someone else—each individual must discover it. If your intention to know yourself is weak, then just a casual wish or hope to change is of very little significance. Without knowing who you are and what habits you need to change, there is no foundation for correct thinking—there is no reality. Without a foundation for correct thinking based upon self-knowledge, there can be no correct action. And without correct action, there can be no change and no way to take your success to the next level.

THE TRUTH WILL SET YOU FREE

You have probably heard the statement "the truth will set you free." The truth begins with an accurate understanding of who and what you are. It's not referring to merely telling the truth, although that's a good place to start, but rather understanding or *seeing* the truth. If you can't see the truth, you are destined to remain stuck in your old ways.

Knowing the truth about yourself is where change begins, taking you to your next level of success. Start with what's real and reality will give you true freedom. Reality comes from understanding *what is* without distortion. When you're working toward reality through a system that someone else has created or through "motivation" or "positive thinking," you are actually postponing understanding reality. You are covering up what is with what you would like it to be. In order to create a new structure for your life and your business success, you must first truly want to be free of your old ways. To move to the next level of success, you must be willing to look at what is and become aware of the limitations you may be placing on yourself.

7

Manage Yourself

How would you like to be truly in control of every aspect of your life? How would you like to not feel at the mercy of external circumstances and not be affected by how others act and respond to you? We've all been programmed to believe that security lies outside us, but it just isn't true. We each create our own security through how we manage our actions and through the choices we make. Self-management starts by making the conscious choice to become the predominant force in your own life. Once that choice is made, you'll have a whole new basis for dealing with the challenges you face in your business and everyday life.

Being a success in any business requires an understanding of some basic principles. The first is decision-making. We are all faced with hundreds, even thousands, of decisions every day. If you want to be successful as an entrepreneur and be financially free, the first decision you must make is to be different. Choose to stand out in the crowd, to do things differently, choose to present yourself to others as a winner who is in control of his or her own destiny. Victims show up thinking they are under the control of someone else's choices, playing someone else's game.

PLAYING CHESS VERSUS CHECKERS

Success is determined by how you play the game. Let's look at the game of checkers as an example. In checkers, you have a board that represents your playing field and twelve checkers, which represent the players in the game. Your opponent has twelve players as well. The objective of the game is to move your players across the playing field, one square at a time in the same direction, and confront your opponent who is doing the same thing. You are both trying to jump your opponent's checkers, eliminating them from the playing field, and trying to keep your own checkers. When you reach the other side of the board, you receive a "crown," which allows you to move in all directions, giving you an edge. You continue until one person has eliminated all the other's players. Pretty simple, huh? Now, compare that to the game of chess. Chess uses the same playing field as checkers, but how many more types of players and moves can be executed in chess? The possibilities are endless, aren't they?

The first step to self-management is to get on the playing field and the second is to realize that you are playing chess not checkers—you have endless moves. The third step is being willing to study all the possible moves and make the right ones. Victims say "I have no choice"; winners say "What's my next move?"

You are faced with making thousands of decisions every day. Some are big decisions, some are small. You decide to get up in the morning, to get dressed, to eat breakfast, to drive to work, to stop at traffic lights. Based upon the decisions you make with clear intention relating to your success, you attract things into your life. But one of the major problems is that we are often too quick to change a decision and go off in another direction. And sometimes we aren't even aware that we've changed our direction, that we are now attracting the things we don't want.

Decision-making can sometimes be like an "inner civil war." It's like being the judge, the attorney, and the jury in your own mental courtroom. You first make a case for yourself. "I am going to make a success out of my business. I am sure I'm right." Then, the prosecuting attorney steps in, "But, your honor, she's not capable of being successful in a business of her own, she's never done it before. In fact, here's concrete evidence—all the past failures she has had." You begin to doubt yourself and your own abilities to be a success, and suddenly you're off track. Your intention has changed. Without even realizing it, you have made a decision to no longer be the predominant force in your own life. You let outside circumstances or past programming make the decision for you.

If you want to succeed, you have to make a firm decision about what you want and then burn the bridge. Pay no attention to the conflicting dialogue that can only pull you off course. Making a conscious decision that takes you in the direction you want to go is the most important step in self-management and in being successful in your business.

AVOID UNDERMINING CHOICES

If your intention is weak, you tend to make poor choices, what I call "undermining choices." Any one of them can be very counterproductive.

First is choice by *limitation,* when you make your decisions based upon what *seems* to be possible but without clear intention. In other words, you limit yourself by your own lack of clear focus on an objective. Or you limit yourself by comparing what you want with your past experience: "I've never owned a business before, therefore I might not succeed."

Second is making a choice by *default.* That's when you say, "Well, I had no other choice, what else could I do?" You give in to circumstances instead of making a decision that will take you where you want to go. You always have another choice; even taking no action at all is a choice and can sometimes be better than taking the wrong action.

Third is making a choice by *condition.*"If this happens, then I'll do this" or "If I can make enough money, then I'll commit to building my business." The key is to reverse the order, because "I'll commit to building my business" is what will bring you the money you need. If you focus your energy on a condition, all you accomplish are more conditions to stop you from being successful. When you make the decision to be successful, you eliminate the condition and move forward with clear intention.

Fourth is making a choice by *reaction,* when you only make decisions that you are forced to because of a crisis. For example, if you get behind on your mortgage payment, then you may go into a panic mode to solve the problem instead of making a decision up front that would eliminate the problem before it happens.

Fifth is making a choice by *consensus,* when you listen to other people's opinions or watch what everyone else does before you decide. This is the reason that many people end up broke at retirement age.

BEING ON PURPOSE WITH A PURPOSE

Here's the key: Decide what you want, then if everyone else wants to follow you, that's fine; if they don't, that's fine as well! Everyone is entitled to an opinion and you should listen to them, but make choices based on your intention—what you want and why. The key to staying on target is "being on purpose with a purpose!" A clear intention is important for two basic reasons: It triggers inspired action that produces results faster and it creates a "structural tension" that pulls you toward your objective.

Having complete clarity is critical to your success and is the foundation of self-management. Clarity is focus, *knowing* where you are going and removing any doubt. Clarity is being on target and on purpose. It is the *fuel* that takes you where you want to go. No matter what business you choose, the speed at which you accomplish your objective will always be based on your own degree of clarity, on your clear intention to succeed. If you take one approach and it doesn't work, you don't quit. You simply take another approach, then another, as many as it takes to get where you want to go. When faced with an obstacle, your clarity of purpose helps you find a way around it, over it, or through it.

If you just can't seem to get going, it means that you aren't clear. Something is holding you back, some obstacle that needs removing or some point that needs clarifying. If you have a fear of talking to people about your product or service, it means that you are not clear about the value of what you have to offer. Your fear blocks your clarity, or your lack of clarity allows fear to creep in, slowing you down. In many cases, fear can even immobilize you. Clarity evaporates fear and connects your *vision* to your *opportunity.* The slightest element of doubt creates uncertainty, and uncertainty always creates lack of clarity. Lack of clarity produces tension, tension produces fear, and fear immobilizes.

Having complete clarity toward what you want means you are living and operating at a higher level of commitment where nothing can interfere with your success. Again, complete clarity means being on purpose with a purpose. An intention to succeed means failure is not an option. Without a clear *intention* to succeed, you won't know where to focus your *attention.* Your actions will become nothing more than "tension relieving" instead of "goal achieving." You'll find yourself involved in more "busyness" instead of business. Whatever you focus your attention on, you will attract, so let your *intention* guide you to where to focus your *attention.* For example, let's say that you are obsessed with your lack of money. What you will attract because of this *is* a lack of money, because that's your focus! If you want wealth, having a clear intention toward being wealthy is absolutely essential. Your clear intention will direct the circumstances in your life to produce the results you desire.

THE LAW OF CAUSE AND EFFECT

Just remember, you will always attract what you project. If you project success, with a clear intention to succeed, you will attract those things that support your success. It's the law of cause and effect, and it will never fail you. It works the same every single time. The law says that you are responsible for creating whatever you attract to yourself. You may or may not like it, but it's a law that can't be broken.

There are three ways by which to base your choices.

First, make no choice at all. Decide not to decide and stay

where you are in your comfort zone, attracting more of the same.

Second, make your choices out of convenience. It's always more convenient:

- Not to make the call.
- Not to take responsibility for your own results.
- Not to say "I'm sorry."
- Not to provide superior customer service.
- Not to attend the meeting.
- Not to eat the right foods to stay healthy.
- Not to improve your skills.
- Not to exercise.
- Not to be self-observant.
- Not to step out of your comfort zone.
- Not to follow through on your commitments.
- Not to be successful.

Convenience is the easy way out. When you decide something out of convenience, what you have really decided is to honor your fear, your comfort zone, or the problem at hand instead of your vision of success.

Third, make the intelligent choices, which will lead you toward your desired outcome. They may not be easy, but I know from experience that failure or just being average are more painful choices than the ones that will lead you toward success.

Your limitations or your accomplishments are always self-imposed by the choices you make, and self-management will be the determining factor in making the right choices. It's not just in making a decision to be wealthy, it's also managing yourself in order to stay on task with your decision. The English politician and author Benjamin Disraeli (1804–1881) once stated, "Nothing can resist the will of a human being who will stake even their existence on the extent of their purpose." Are you willing to stake your existence on what you believe in?

LOOK FOR THE TRUTH

Self-management calls for looking for the real truth behind every situation, and the only method I know of for gaining truth is being more observant. Truth simply means *seeing* versus *not seeing*. It means being in touch with what's going on around you as opposed to having your view clouded by your own prejudices or by the beliefs and thoughts of those around you.

If you drop a frog into boiling water, it will immediately jump out. On the other hand, it is said that if you place a frog into lukewarm water and then gradually raise the temperature to a boil, it will stay there until it dies. Unlike a frog, you have the capacity to *see* when you are slipping too far into "hot water," into an unhealthy situation or a nonproductive state of mind. You can stop, observe the situation, and decide if you want to proceed or take a different, more productive direction. That's called self-management. You need to realize that you're the one striking the match and lighting your own fire! This can only be done, however, if you are willing to see the reality of the situation, then act on what you know to be the truth. "This water it getting hot and it's time to get out!" No one can learn the truth from another—you must resolve to see the truth, to see reality as it is.

Let's say that you are driving your car down the road at high speed and suddenly you see another car in your lane coming directly at you. A head-on collision is about to happen if you don't act fast. What do you do? Are you going to take the time and weigh the pros and cons of continuing on your collision course? Are you going to think, "Well, he's on my side of the road and if he hits me, it will be his fault." No, of course not! If you're faced with a head-on collision, you're not going to contemplate the situation, you are going to act. You have no other choice, do you? You see the truth, you see reality, and you take action.

Seeing the truth means not being trapped by any one particular point of view, a prisoner of your own or someone else's beliefs. Just because you "believe" something doesn't mean that it is true. You may believe that the other driver is in the wrong and is going to get out of your way, but is that true? Are you willing to risk your life and trust your belief? Seeing the truth acknowledges what is actually happening at that moment and then taking appropriate action, if needed. When a problem arises, don't ask "What do I believe?" or "What do I do now?" but rather "What do I need to understand? What is the truth?" As an entrepreneur, if you find that the water is getting too hot, you may have to act quickly.

Whether you see your current situation or a problem as a hardship or as an opportunity depends on your point of view, not on your circumstances. Being successful in any endeavor requires that you remain conscious of what's going on around you and inside of you, in your own thinking, beliefs, feelings, and actions. When you are feeling fearful, if you look inside, you'll see the reasons for your fear. You'll see that your fears are simply a series of recurring thoughts, feelings, and emotions, which are a mirror of how you believe your situation should or should not be. Your fear may also be rooted in how you believe others should or shouldn't be acting, how things used to be in your past, how you expect the future to be, or how you can manipulate people and your circumstances to get what you want. None of these factors have anything to do with what's really happening right now, and that's the only thing that truly matters. This moment is the only thing that's real, so look for the truth in it. Seeing the truth creates reality, it lets you see the reality behind your actions as well as which actions to take.

In order to make permanent change, begin to observe how you feel or react in an uncomfortable situation or when you are faced with a problem or a difficult decision. Begin to notice how you act in your relationships with others, how you act in a crowd, how you act at work or even when you relax. If you want to make rapid advancement personally and professionally, there is nothing about yourself that shouldn't be observed. If you want to know the truth, if you want to know reality, constantly observe yourself.

Now, don't make this too complicated. You don't have to stop everything you're doing just to observe yourself. You may be surprised at your discoveries—you may find yourself being uptight when you try to relax or feeling uncomfortable when you are around someone who is more financially successful than you. Any aspect of yourself that you don't observe will remain obscure to you. Without self-observation, everything will always seem to be outside your control. But when you honestly observe yourself, you'll begin to see that you are in total control of how you feel in any given situation. By observing, you can figure out your own nonproductive programming.

Develop the habit of checking in with yourself before taking action as well as while taking action. *There is no reality in the absence of observation. Observation creates reality.* If you don't seek the truth behind your actions, you could be taking actions that lead you away from your desired results. For example, you may say that you can't get enough customers to stay in business. But with further examination, you may discover that you are not willing to step out of your own comfort zone and do something in a different way to expand your customer base.

Often in sales—which we are all in, in one way or the other—we try to control the outcome. In reality, we should focus on making a better presentation that shows the benefit to the buyer. An outcome is simply an outcome, and the more you try to control it, the less control you actually have over it.

WHAT YOU ATTEMPT TO CONTROL, CONTROLS YOU

Imagine for a moment that you are standing in the middle of the freeway between two lanes of traffic. There are cars and trucks about a foot from you on either side, traveling at 80 miles per hour. You probably wouldn't feel very comfortable there, would you? In fact, you would more than likely feel immobilized and afraid to move at all. You are aware of where you are, and you don't like it—that's called self-awareness.

What if you were to step up on the median strip and observe the traffic from there? It wouldn't feel quite so intimidating, would it? You would still be "aware" of the traffic, but from a slightly higher viewpoint. What if you backed off a little further and observed the traffic from a helicopter 500 feet in the air—it would even appear a lot less threatening, wouldn't it? And if you observed the traffic from a mile high in an airplane, it would look like a colored ribbon woven through the landscape. From that level of observation, it wouldn't seem like a threat at all, would it? That's called observation or seeing the truth.

Self-awareness is knowing you're in it, whereas self-observation is separating yourself from it, so you can see the real issue. Now, you can either accept it for what it is or take appropriate action to make a change.

Often, we get so caught up in our problems that we develop tunnel vision. We can't see anything but the problem and become consumed by it. We are definitely aware of it, but when you're consumed by the problem you have no capacity to find a solution. When you observe with a panoramic view, you start to see the traffic or any other problem you face for what it is—just a problem that needs solving—not something out to get you. You just need to rise above it and observe it from another viewpoint.

When faced with a problem, many people believe themselves to be victims of some sort of cruel fate. We put off facing our difficult tasks, because we are always swinging back and forth between conformity and nonconformity. For example, you arrive at work one morning and know that you have a difficult issue that you need to deal with, one that you really don't want to confront. Later, in the afternoon, you suddenly realize that you still haven't done it. You've found fifty things to do, none of which confront the issue at hand.

Your initial response upon arriving at work was that you

should deal with it immediately. You're the boss and it's your job. That's conformity. Your next response was that you are the boss, so you don't have to deal with it or you can do it later. That's nonconformity. And the instant you step back, observe both sides, and begin to see what you're really doing, which is putting off a difficult task and wasting valuable time and energy, you confront the issue.

However, if you never take the time to observe, you may put off taking any action at all. In fact, without observation, you may not even realize that you're putting it off in the first place. But with self-observation, you see through and understand the maze you're caught up in. By being observant, you'll see what you're *really* doing—wasting time and energy—and you'll see a resourceful solution. You'll begin to see how you swing between conformity and nonconformity, caught between a resourceful and nonresourceful state and watching your precious moments tick by. And by becoming more self-observant, you'll begin to realize that you are the one pushing your own swing.

The solution is to face the truth and resolve the problem by facing what you don't want to experience. Get it done and move on! When you simply surrender to the experience, everything will begin to shift, allowing you to see clearly what needs to be done.

YOU, INCORPORATED

Keep in mind that as an entrepreneur, you are sometimes both the employer as well as the employee. Look at it this way: I, Inc. hires You, Inc. I, Inc. then tells You, Inc. what to do, what your job description is. You, Inc. then commits to I, Inc. to do the job that I, Inc. directed You, Inc. to do. And if You, Inc. doesn't do the job, then I, Inc. should call a meeting with You, Inc. to find out why. At the meeting, I, Inc. should help You, Inc. to re-clarify your job description and to again define clearly what action steps You, Inc. should take to get the job done. Then, if You, Inc. fails to meet the expectations set forth by I, Inc., then I, Inc. calls another meeting with You, Inc. to let You, Inc. know it is being fired for lack of performance.

Begin today to observe yourself, the I, Inc. and the You, Inc. Begin to "let go" of nonproductive programming and habit patterns in order to make room for new solutions. Begin today to take more action, more often. Take responsibility, not for how or why your programs and patterns got developed or what you are experiencing as a result, but for changing what needs changing. Nothing else matters in the least if you don't look for the truth in your situation and then take full responsibility for your own success.

Instead of asking "How do I relieve my anxiety?" observe the feeling and then ask yourself "What feeling am I hanging on to that's causing me to feel anxious?" Instead of saying "Why is this person acting this way?" observe reality and then ask yourself "Why should I suffer over how someone else acts?" Their actions are their own problem, not yours, unless their actions negatively affect your business. And if you've tried everything you know to resolve their problem, you can simply make a choice to no longer do business with them.

Your attitude toward a problem will determine the outcome, so it is vitally important to develop an aspiring and resourceful attitude. The following aspirations would be helpful.

- Aspire to do well in your business and you'll find solutions to do so.
- Aspire to give good service and your customers will return.
- Aspire to assist your team and your business will prosper.
- Aspire to help others and they will support your success.
- Aspire to have people like you and they will.
- Aspire to be nonjudgmental toward yourself and others and you'll feel better about yourself and others.
- Aspire to have people listen to you and you'll develop better communication skills.
- Aspire to present yourself well and people will want to listen.

- Aspire to become a good listener and you'll discover more clearly your customers' needs.

- Aspire to have people love your product or service and they'll beat a path to your door.

More times than not, you'll get exactly what you "aspire" to have in your life. The results of self-management through seeing the truth will always show up on the bottom line, in the success of your business. Right now, you are capable of dramatically improving your performance. You can multiply your personal effectiveness, hit new heights in your business and financial affairs, and shatter your old achievement records. I don't want you to believe me—try it and see for yourself. The results that you could achieve will be hard for you to imagine until you get there.

You don't have to settle for things as they are now, the status quo. Your life can change dramatically at any moment you choose to make a change. Your choices will dictate the change. If you are ready for it, observing your actions will give you a breakthrough experience. You can enjoy a completely different plane of success, and as your level of performance improves drastically, so will your rate of accomplishments. You haven't been reaching your full potential up to this point—you haven't even come close! No matter how you define achievement, you have barely scratched the surface of what you can accomplish. But maybe the time has come for you to change all that. Are you ready for that giant leap forward?

8

A Strategy for Success

Imagine being in a hotel conference room for a meeting you are conducting. You arrive early to set up the room and as you enter, you discover that it is pitch black—there are no lights on. What would you do? Of course, your answer would be, "Turn on the lights!" But what if you didn't know where the light switch was located, then what would you do? You would more than likely feel around on the wall to see if you could locate the switch. Would you feel around at one foot above the floor or one foot from the ceiling? "No, that would be silly," you might say. The reason is that you already know, based on past experience, that the switch is almost always located about four feet above the floor beside the door. But what if you feel your way around the wall and still don't locate the switch, what would your next strategy be? You might find a maintenance person or call the sales office for help, wouldn't you?

My point is that you wouldn't walk into the room and expect the lights to go on automatically, would you? You would have a strategy for turning on the lights. And if step one didn't work, you would move to step two and so on. The same holds true with a business. You wouldn't start a business and expect it to succeed without a plan to begin, would you? I'm not talking about a five-year plan or even a one-year plan, just a plan to get started. You have invested a substantial amount of money into your business and now you are going to feel your way around in the dark hoping that someday it will work? That would be ridiculous, wouldn't it?

INTRODUCE PEOPLE TO YOUR PRODUCT OR SERVICES

I had a meeting one day that changed my life and my business forever. A vice president from the company I was involved with asked me, "What is your strategy for being successful in your business?" My response was, "Get rid of all this soap that fills my garage and home." Then, he asked me how I planned to do that, and my reply was, "I don't know."

He explained that every business owner should have a business strategy portfolio. A business strategy portfolio is your strategy for building your business. Would you start a business without a plan for success? I did, and at the end of the first year in business, I was not doing well at all. The thought of filing for bankruptcy had occurred to me, but the problem was I didn't even have enough money to do that.

The vice president said, "Let's begin with your job description. If someone asks you what it is you do, what would you tell them?"

My first response was, "I sell soap." My next response was, "I recruit people for a business opportunity." I went on with other possibilities: "I change people's lives," etc.

He asked me once again, "If someone asked you to write your job description, what would it say? Every business owner should have one."

He asked, "What do teachers do?" I said, "They teach school."

"And what do pilots do?" he asked. I said, "They fly planes."

He went on, "And what do carpenters do?" "They drive nails," I said.

"What about taxi drivers?" he asked. "They drive taxis."

"Correct," he said. "And if teachers don't teach, taxi drivers don't drive, pilots don't fly, and carpenters don't drive nails, what do you suppose happens?" I said, "They don't get paid."

"And what do you do?" he asked once again. I still couldn't

come up with the answer. After a year in a business, I didn't even know my job description!

"Your job description is this," he said. And I'll never forget these words: "Your job description is *to talk to people every day about your products or your business opportunity and teach others to do the same.* There's a simple success formula: If you talk a little, you earn a little, and if you talk a lot, you earn a lot. If you aren't talking to people every day about your business or your opportunity and teaching those you enroll to do the same, you are not in business! If there is a day that goes by that you don't do this, you had your doors closed for business that day. And that's okay if you want to close your doors for a day, but when you do, you also have to understand that you won't do any business, so don't expect to get paid for something you do not do."

No matter what business you may have chosen, the lifeblood of the business is introducing people to your product or service. If you let a day go by that you don't do this, that's one day you're closed for business. If you introduce a lot, you will earn a lot; if you introduce a little, you will earn a little. How you choose to introduce them to your product is up to you, but the more you introduce, the more you get paid.

He said, "If you want to be successful, you have to have a mind-set that you're in business for yourself, you're in business to make money, and you're in business to make money daily."

He asked me how much I wanted to earn every day. I finally decided that I wanted one hundred dollars a day to start. He then said, "Well, someone out there has your hundred dollars."

And I asked, "Who is it?"

He said, "Oh, you'll know them."

"How?" I asked.

He said, "When they give you the hundred dollars, that's how." Finally, he said, "If you don't have a mind-set that you're in business to make at least one hundred dollars a day, you won't put forth the effort to talk to enough people to find the one with a hundred dollars who is willing to part with it for your products."

Sometimes I hear people complaining, "My business isn't working." The question should be, "How many people did you expose your product to today?" And "How many of your team (if you have a team) did you teach to do the same?" What about yesterday and what about your plan for tomorrow? Anyone who *is not* exposing his or her product to people on a daily basis will soon be saying, "This business doesn't work." Why? Because it won't work unless you introduce others to your product, and that requires a strategy.

REFINING YOUR APPROACH

When I first set up my website, I decided on a great name—www.personalgrowthtips.com—as I thought there would be a lot of people surfing the web interested in personal growth. I knew a lot about my product and believed in it strongly. I knew that everyone needed what I had to offer, but marketing on the internet was new to me.

I spent a great deal of money and time constructing my website, several months in fact. After all that effort, I was excited to finally launch it and was very excited about the possibilities that the internet provided. The next day, I went online to collect all my orders, and to my surprise there were none. I was disappointed but I thought I must have caught everyone on an off day. I waited for two more days and still had no orders. I thought, "Maybe it takes some time to get noticed and for people to find your site." I waited another week, then a month, and guess what? Still no orders! Talk about rejection. I thought, "There are hundreds of millions of people on the internet and no one wants my products."

What I didn't know was the job description for marketing on the internet. I knew I had to reach people to sell my products, but I didn't know the correct strategy for reaching them online. I didn't know that it was my responsibility to drive traffic to my site—I thought they would just find me because I had an excellent product. I didn't know that I had to get exposure on the big internet search engines. In fact, I didn't even know what a search engine was!

You don't want to spend all your time planning to get started, but you do have to have a starting point for exposing your product to potential buyers. I wanted to get exposure on the internet, but I found out right away that my plan needed to change.

Strategy is like a mind-set, just like success is a mind-set, to do certain things every day that earn you money. To earn money requires a strategy to get your product in front of potential buyers. And if one approach doesn't work, take another, and then another, until you find one that does work. Remember, a plan is not something that you stick with no matter what. If you've given it ample time to work and it's not working, change it. You either prove that it works or you prove that it doesn't work. And when you find something that works, do more of it.

If you have a clear strategy for exposing your product to potential customers, when you retire for the evening, you can do one of two things—you can celebrate a job well done or you can make corrections. If the approach you took today didn't work, try another one tomorrow. Without some form of a strategy plan, you have nothing to celebrate and nothing to correct. Continually ask yourself, "How can I get the best return on my investment from my strategy plan?" For example, if you've invested money into building a website to market your product, the first question you should ask yourself is, "How can I get the fastest and the largest return on my dollars invested?" To get a return, you have to "fill the pipeline" with information flowing to your prospects. If you fill the pipeline, you'll get results coming out the other end. Filling the pipeline simply means getting maximum exposure for your product.

Success is determined by what you do on a daily basis that earns you the right to success. Again, the key word is *earn.* You have to earn success, and you earn it by introducing people to your product every day. The more you introduce, the more you earn. Did you fill the pipeline today with information flowing to new prospects? If not, why not? Because without filling the pipeline, a few days from now there will be no follow-up, and no sales.

In order to be successful at any level, you must be clear about the following:

1. You're in business for yourself and you have to treat it like a business.

2. You're the boss. You have to set up your own business strategy plan, policies, and procedures, and stick to them.

3. You must have a mind-set to follow a plan that earns you money daily.

If a person doesn't do well, it often simply means that he or she didn't expect much in the first place, he or she didn't have a strategy plan that guided him or her toward success, or the person didn't follow the strategy plan.

So, the bottom line is: Develop a clear strategy plan, expose your product or service to a lot of people, be real nice, give good service, have a lot of fun, celebrate your successes, never give up, and your business will grow and prosper. Along the way, your plans can and most likely will change. When many people hit obstacles, the first thing they sacrifice is their goal, not the plan. They get hooked on the plan, almost addicted to it. If a plan is not working, high achievers change the plan, not their goal.

A Plan is Only an Approximation of Reality

As an entrepreneur, one of the first things to realize is that a plan is simply an approximation of reality, not necessarily reality itself. It's not the goal—a plan is simply a track to run on that will get you to your goal, a vehicle that may or may not change along the way. Your plan begins the process of taking your goal from the idea stage into physical reality. It acts as an energy magnet or a goal generator to boost your power. The very act of having a plan, a starting place, a track to begin your journey, is the only way you get on the road toward your chosen objective. And it will provide you ample opportunity to make course corrections along the way.

Also, once you execute your plan it becomes an act of vulnerability and commitment that may challenge some old beliefs that need changing. When this happens, it will present to you a time of choice and of course correction. Course corrections will allow you to maintain "intentional focus" toward your desired outcome. In other words, you'll always be looking for new and better ways of achieving the end result.

CATCHING THE RIGHT TRENDS

Part of your strategy should be to follow a trend. In fact, if possible you want to be in front of a coming trend. If you can predict a trend and get in front of it with the right product, it will literally push you to success. It's like riding a giant wave. The housing market in the 1970s, the SUV market in the 1980s, the computer boom of the 1980s and 1990s, the dot com and internet explosion in the 1990s and 2000s were all trends. Trends can make you rich if you get in on the right one at the right time.

Let me offer you some other examples. How many people carried a cell phone twenty years ago? The answer is almost no one. How many people had cell phones ten years ago? Some, but still very few. And today?—almost everyone. That's a trend. Twenty years ago, how many households owned a VCR? About 20 percent. How about ten years ago? The answer is about 85 percent. How many own VCRs today? The answer is almost no one! Why? Because the trend changed to DVD players—now, over 85 percent of households own two or more DVD players.

What's next? If you can predict a trend and get in front of it, you can get rich. Who would have thought that a coffeehouse selling designer coffees at five dollars a cup would expand to thousands of locations. Starbucks is one of the greatest small business success stories today! Look at almost any industry or product and ask yourself, "What's next?" Let's look at a rising trend. As baby boomers continue to age, the U.S. Census Bureau predicts that the senior market (those ages sixty and over) will grow by 81 percent over the next twenty-five years. Here are some tips that would help you ride the wave of this exploding trend.

Forget the stereotypical senior. Today's seniors are a new breed, as diverse as the rest of the population. They are more active and healthier than previous generations and they have more money to spend. In fact, according to a recent issue of *Senior Magazine,* the senior population controls 70 percent of the nation's disposable income! They also account for more than 25 percent of toy and children's clothing purchases, over 40 percent of new car purchases, and more than 80 percent of luxury travel expenditures.

You'll find them shopping online. In recent years, most of the population has been flocking to the internet to shop for better prices when making their purchases. It is estimated that the senior market alone made purchases on the internet totaling more than seven billion dollars in 2002. They are also the fastest growing segment of internet users, according to Neilsen/NetRatings. From 2002 to 2003, the number of seniors over sixty-five using the internet rose 25 percent, and use among those fifty-five to sixty-four rose more than 15 percent. As more and more internet-savvy consumers reach retirement, that number will continue to grow.

They want to be informed. Seniors want to be better informed before making a decision than other consumers. They are not willing to part with their hard-earned money unless they are sure they are making a wise decision. Therefore, providing more quality and quantity of information will encourage them to make their purchases.

They are loyal. Seniors are known to be brand-loyal: They want to feel valued as a customer, and if they feel valued by a company, they will continue to buy and be loyal. Not only that, they'll tell their friends! If you are going after a share of this trend, you'll want to connect with them on a more personal level, with honesty and sincerity. They don't want to be talked down to or be patronized. You'll want to think of them as a long-term customer rather than just a quick sale.

THE HOME-BASED BUSINESS TREND

One rising trend is working from home—owning a home-based

business and having a second income. Millions of people are gravitating toward starting their own home-based business and many are making more money than they ever dreamed possible. And they're doing it without the commute, without leasing expensive offices, without hiring employees, and so on.

Home-based business is an industry whose time has come. Whether you are offering a product around the world through the use of the World Wide Web or to your neighbor next door, home-based businesses are building bridges between research, technology, state-of-the-art products, consumer goods, and the needs and demands of society. Having your own business at home is similar to the visionaries who brought the wagon and the internal combustion engine together to create an automobile. The home-based business trend is creating the success stories of this decade, and professionals from all walks of life have found greater success. In fact, it's happening to someone just like you this very minute.

In my entrepreneur training workshops, I've met doctors, carpenters, attorneys, writers, accountants, factory workers, teachers, every profession you could imagine, and even high-school dropouts, who are thriving in a business they created from home. For example, I met a former chiropractor and his wife selling legal services who, after eighteen months, were earning in excess of twenty thousand dollars a month; a twenty-five-year-old factory worker earning ten thousand dollars a month in the telephone service business; a retired husband-and-wife team, after one year, were earning over twelve thousand dollars each month marketing cosmetics; a seventy-four-year-old grandmother earning six thousand dollars a month; and a former cattle rancher earning over fifty thousand dollars a month in a nutritional business.

We're living in the most affluent economy ever and lucrative opportunities are all around us. Yet, most people are still living paycheck to paycheck, working longer and longer hours just to stay even. Why? Because they bought into the wrong plan, that's why. They've fallen into the "time for money" trap, and that's not the way to get ahead financially. There are a multitude of opportunities that offer you a chance—no matter what your background, education, or experience—to create a thriving business of your own right from your home.

THE RISE OF NETWORK MARKETING

A big part of the trend in the home-based business revolution is an industry known as network marketing. Now, I know that a lot of people have negative feelings about network marketing, but that's because they don't understand it. Network marketing is a smart way to start a business at a low cost, usually for under a thousand dollars. You have virtually no risk. The real difference between other businesses and network marketing is that in networking you invest your time and energy instead of your money. With a year of concentrated effort—a few hours a day, part time—you can build a substantial business that can set you free financially, and you can even start turning a profit after the first month or two. That's unheard of in traditional business.

The trouble is that many people, because they want instant gratification, don't really have the determination, the mental toughness, or the stamina to stick with it long enough to make it work. Besides, often they have friends or family who have negative beliefs about network marketing: It didn't work for them or Uncle Ralph had a bad experience. In my opinion, that's "the language of the poor." Just because Uncle Ralph wasn't successful does not mean that it doesn't work—it means that Uncle Ralph didn't have the determination to make it work.

If you want to get ahead, you have to open your mind and change some of the ways you look at things and not allow poverty-minded people to influence you. If someone advises you about your financial future, about whether or not you should start a business of any type, make sure that they are qualified to make the recommendations. Everyone has an opinion about almost everything, but is it worth listening to? There's nothing wrong with network marketing; the failure rate is no higher than in any other type of business. Network marketing is where I got my start in the late

1960s and early 1970s, and it was a valid way then and now to build toward financial freedom. For the average person with not much money to invest, it can be a great business. In fact, it's the trend for today's small business builder. When I started, I had nine dollars in the bank and I turned it into financial freedom.

The problem is that the average person doesn't consider network marketing to be a real business. My question is this: "How would the average person who's never done well in any kind of business know what a real business is?" So, why would you listen to their advice?

If you took five hundred dollars and placed it in a savings account, what interest do you suppose you would earn? Somewhere between one and two percent, or about $7.50 a year. And if you had to drive to the bank to make the deposit, you would probably lose money the first year. On the other hand, you could join a network marketing company and invest that five hundred dollars into some tools to build a business. Most companies have CDs, DVDs, and other materials available for you to hand out to people you meet, which explain the value of the products and the opportunity available.

Let's say, for example, that for five hundred dollars you could get five hundred CDs. And over the next year, you handed out all those CDs. What percentage of the people do you think might be interested in your business or product? The answer I get most often is 20 percent. Well, if that 20 percent becomes a part of your team—that's one hundred people. If each person used or sold only a thousand dollars a year in commissionable products, that's a total sales volume of $100,000 for the year.

If you earned only 10 percent of that total, you would be earning ten thousand dollars a year. Sure, you put forth some effort, but you are now starting to leverage your time and your money. Where else can you get that sort of return that fast on five hundred dollars? That's a twentyfold return on your investment! But you also build a residual income because a great number of those customers continue to use your product year after year while you build the next group.

The great thing about network marketing is that the people you sponsor to be business partners with you start to duplicate your efforts by doing the same as you, producing leveraged effort and income. In network marketing, you build a network of distributors and customers who are also building a network of distributors and customers, causing your business and income potential to grow month after month. In the beginning, you put in more time and effort than you are getting paid for, but later on, because of the effort of your network, you are getting paid for much more than the effort you are putting forth. I know people who have, within a few years, built a network of over 10,000 people or more and are earning residual incomes of hundreds of thousands of dollars a year.

Network marketing is a viable vehicle if you find the right company and you stick with it long enough to make it work. I have been exposed to many network companies over the years and I've met tens of thousands of people who are thriving in the industry. If you would like an introduction to some viable companies, you can e-mail me at info@jimbritt.com. You can also review the training I offer specifically for network marketers at the website www.networkmarketing1.com.

The world is changing, and if you want financial freedom, you have to change with it. If you want to be successful, you can no longer allow unsuccessful people and outdated thinking to influence you. If you want financial freedom, you have to be willing to do whatever it takes to have it and, most importantly, that includes making your own decisions about what you do or don't do, whether or not others agree with you. Freedom simply means you have more choices. If you have a regular salaried job, you've probably given up a lot of your freedom. There's nothing wrong with a regular job, unless you want freedom, then everything is wrong with it, because you are helping someone else accomplish his or her goals. You're playing someone else's game instead of being the maker of your own game!

In a normal job, somebody tells you how much money you

make, when you come to work, when you get a pay raise, and even when to retire—or in some cases that you no longer have a job or a retirement! I'm not interested in having somebody tell me how much money I can make or whether or not I have a job tomorrow. With very little cash to invest in a business, the average person has an option with network marketing that you might not otherwise have. You could be on your way toward achieving financial freedom for an investment of under one thousand dollars. Where else can you do that?

YOU'VE GOT TO BE BOLD

If you want to survive in today's world, you have to be bold. You have to be willing to put yourself out there and take some risks. And the first step, in my opinion, is reclaiming your own freedom at whatever cost. There are many people who go to work every day to a job that they hate. They stay because they want job security, but there's no security in a job. If you want to get better, you have to be bold, to be willing to step out of your comfort zone. You've got to stop working for someone else's dreams and start working for your own.

Most people don't have the education for success—they don't teach success principles in college. Network marketing gives you a vehicle where you can get educated as you grow your business. What a great deal that is! If you want to be successful in network marketing, it's really not that difficult. I have trained and coached tens of thousands of people and all you have to do is apply a few basic principles daily and then give it time to work. In fact, my book and CDs, *Money: How to Earn It, How to Make It Grow,* was written specifically for the network marketing industry. You can also take what you learn in this book and put it into action.

A friend of mine has been in network marketing for five years. For the first four years, he built his business, working a few hours a day, to a substantial income of six figures a year. During the last year, his business has grown more than in the first four years. Because of the exponential growth through the efforts of his network, his income has doubled in the last twelve months. Today, he makes more than five hundred thousand dollars a year, and he did it with a five hundred dollar investment and some "sweat equity."

If you're wondering if your job will be there tomorrow or if you'll get a pay raise, you have lost your freedom and you need to do something about it. I'm not trying to sell you on network marketing, but if you don't have another entrepreneurial idea or a lot of money to invest in starting a business, it's the best vehicle I know of. Network marketing provides the freedom, the mentorship, the training, and the support—it's like being in business for yourself but not by yourself. And everyone above you in the company wants you to succeed because it's to their advantage to help you build your business. Their success is determined by your success. I call it "enlightened capitalism."

Most people dream dreams that will never happen. The truth is that a person can easily dream of making a million dollars, but most people are never going to do it because they are not willing to go through the discipline and the discomfort of changing. To become financially free, you need more than a dream—you need a plan, a system, a vehicle to take you where you want to go. I have been involved in many entrepreneurial ventures over the years, representing many different industries. I started off in a network marketing business, and it was very good to me. If I had to do it all again, I would choose network marketing as a way to get started in my own business. For the average person, a network marketing business provides a chance for some control over his or her life and financial future. If you'll give it some concentrated effort for a period of time, it will work. A network marketing business simply gives you more choices, and if you have more choices, you have more freedom. That's what this country was founded upon, the freedom to choose.

There will always be the friend or the relative who says, "Why are you in the network marketing business? That kind of business doesn't work." Well, all I can say is that if you let that person make your decisions, then you're the one who loses. The best thing about network marketing is that if you can stick with it, work at it for just a couple hours a day even for a year or so, you will become a completely different person. Even if you don't earn a dime, you will become a changed person just from the education you'll receive. A person has to get tougher and smarter if they want to get ahead financially. And I think that's what network marketing offers—the opportunity to get tougher and smarter and earn a lot of money at the same time, with little or no risk.

ALL OPPORTUNITIES ARE NOT CREATED EQUAL

All companies and network marketing opportunities are not created equal. Let me offer you the five elements that make up a great business opportunity in that industry.

The right trend and timing. The industry, the trend, and the product or service upon which the opportunity is based must be growing, dynamic, and exciting to the end user. Radio used to be the popular means of home entertainment, then television came along and took over the market. Radio is still around and still popular today, but the opportunity is no longer as big as it was. So, it's important to be in front of, or at least in the middle of, a trend. If you are behind it, it may not be as exciting to the consumer or your team as it should be, and not as profitable either.

Outstanding products or services. Your product must be in high demand by a large number of people. As I stated earlier, the baby boomers represent the biggest buying audience of the future. What do you think they want? Well, they want to live longer, feel better, have more energy, look better, be more informed, more comfortable, and travel more. They are looking for high-quality, proven products that will help them achieve their chosen lifestyle.

High profit potential. You want to get paid well for your efforts. If you provide exceptional products, you should be rewarded exceptionally for your efforts. So, you want to be sure that the margin of profit is high enough for the products offered.

Tools and support. If your chosen business happens to be part of a bigger company on which you rely, such as franchising or network marketing, you should expect to be provided with the tools, training, and support that you need to succeed.

A stable company with high integrity. If you are connected to a parent company, a great opportunity can go bad if your company or its leadership goes bad. If you are going to invest your money and your time, get the assurance that you are dealing with a company whose people show commitment, capability, and integrity.

Determine what you want to accomplish. You have to measure what you want to accomplish against the opportunity, and then decide if the opportunity will take you where you want to go financially. Only you can decide what it is you want, and only you can decide what opportunity is right.

CREATE A NEW FUTURE

The real events in life are in the choices you make—each one creates a new future. Today grew out of yesterday's choices, and tomorrow will grow out of today's. Make a choice to be financially free. Remember, being stuck in your current circumstances or living financially free require the same three ingredients: intention, willingness, and commitment. Take action today—learn the skills covered in this book and put them to use immediately! If you are not already involved in your own business, get one started. Get fully involved with your chosen opportunity and soon you'll be on your way to having the personal and financial freedom you've always dreamed of having.

9

Build Lasting Relationships

Many years ago, I found a small vitamin store located in a strip mall in southern California. Alongside it was a supermarket, a large drugstore chain, a clothing chain store, and a few other small shops. The store was about the size of a single car garage and was filled wall-to-wall with vitamins, with the exception of a very small fresh juice bar in the corner. I began visiting the store frequently to purchase my vitamins and herbs. The owner, Bruce, had the best prices going. His inspiration for starting his own business was that he was buying vitamins up the street one day and realized how high their prices were, so he decided to start his own vitamin store and offer the same products at a discount.

I was away for a few months, but when I returned, the size of Bruce's store had doubled. About a year later, it doubled again, then again and again, until it was about the same size as the large drugstore next door. A few years later, he opened a second store, then a third. One day, I asked Bruce what he thought was the major key to his success. He answered by saying that he provided his customers with what they wanted and built his store around their needs and requests.

When he first opened his store, a woman from a nearby city came in and asked for a certain vitamin. He told her that he didn't carry the line but that he would get it for her and call her when it came in. A week or so later, the small bottle of vitamins arrived and Bruce placed a long-distance call to the woman to let her know. One of her kids answered and didn't pass on the message. A few days later, he called and left a message on her message machine. On his third try, Bruce finally talked to the woman. When she picked up the product, which sold for only $1.75, he mentioned that he had ordered additional bottles, which would be there when she needed them. I asked him how he could place a special order and make three long-distance calls for a product that had only about a 75-cent profit margin. I said, "You must have lost money on the deal." He explained that he didn't just sell her a product—he was really working on developing long-term customer loyalty.

That was how his store was created. Bruce said that you could never duplicate his store because it was made up of thousands of individuals' needs and requests. He filled the individual needs of each customer knowing that whether the first purchase was one dollar or twenty dollars didn't really matter. He looked at the long-term potential: Over time, that small purchase would turn into higher profits generated from more purchases.

As he expanded into selling organic vegetables and fruits, an organic restaurant, a bookstore, and other products that you couldn't find anywhere else, my family and I spent well over fifteen hundred dollars every month in Bruce's store. And we weren't alone. The rumor was that he was doing more business in his health food store than all the large chain stores combined that neighbored him in the mall.

THE SECRET TO SUCCESS

The secret to success in any business is to provide an excellent product and to give your customers excellent service. Some of the decisions that will need to be made may seem unprofitable to you at the time. In fact, some decisions may actually lose you money in the short term, but you are creating the potential to yield excellent long-term profits. The bottom line is that without customers eventually there is no company. There has to be a final consumer for the product, otherwise the company cannot remain in business. And if you don't develop customer loyalty for future repeat business, you may not be in business very long either. Customer loyalty starts with developing a relationship with your customer.

You don't need to be an expert in order to sell your product. Almost every business I've started was because I thought it was a great idea and I believed that there was a viable market and a need for my product. I was not an expert in the field and in many cases I had no experience at all in a particular area. In order to stay in business, you have to satisfy your customers' needs, which involves much more than just providing a product. When a person is no longer willing to pay for what you provide, you're out of business. And being an expert won't change that, not even a little bit. What you do need to be an expert at is providing a benefit to your customer and building a relationship through great customer service.

The key to a successful product is to do the proper upfront investigation and research. Get an idea, make up a sample product, and then take the sample product to potential customers to get their feedback. Then, keep doing that "fine-tune and get input" loop until you believe you have a winner or until you decide that it isn't something worth pursuing.

Years ago, I was involved with a perfume company as a marketing consultant. They produced perfumes that were similar to original designer brands but using better quality ingredients. In double-blind studies, their perfumes came out the winner over 95 percent of the time. However, even though the price of their product was only 20 percent of what the competition charged, most people still didn't want to buy it. The company owner didn't give up. Their next step was to create and sell "the sizzle," the appeal of the bottle and packaging. They hired *the* premier bottle designer in France and created a look that won an International Design Award. They did another double-blind study and again they were chosen over the designer fragrances 95 percent of the time, but now people also wanted to make a purchase. They had three benefits that put them ahead of the competition: quality, packaging, and price. The designer fragrance sold for four hundred dollars an ounce, while their product sold for about eighty dollars an ounce, was of higher quality, and it looked more appealing.

One of the keys to success is to find out who your customers are and then listen to them. Let them have a "thumbprint" on your product. By doing so, you will have a better product and you will also have the most important thing you can have—a working relationship with your customers. They will guide you toward success. To become and remain successful, you will also have to constantly reinvent yourself and maybe even your product. You do that, in part, by listening to and following your customers' lead. Consider where the automobile, airlines, building materials, and any other product or service industry would be without reinventing their product or approach to the market as needs and demands of consumers have changed. Just remember, you are in business to fill a customer's need, not just to sell a product.

You can start by brainstorming customer needs and product links. Once you've decided what it is you want to market, get the creative juices flowing by creating a list of potential customers and learn to translate from "what you want to sell" to "what they want to hear." For example, let's say you are selling music CDs and your target is the high school student. Maybe discount prices are what they want to hear or maybe you are selling the convenience of shopping online and reducing the cost by leaving out the middleman.

Also, start to brainstorm the marketplace. What are people looking for today? What are the trends and what products are hot? What products that were once hot are now tapering off a bit? And even more important, what will replace that product? Look at a marketplace and ask yourself what the market will be looking for in the near future. Teen market, baby boomers, college students, parents, education, technology—which one do you want to serve? Begin to look ahead, because if you want to do well, you'll want to get in front of a coming trend.

CLIMB INTO YOUR CUSTOMER'S POINT OF VIEW

When you come up with an idea, begin to list the benefits that a customer might expect from your product. Climb into your customer's point of view and look at your product from his or her angle. You'll begin to discover many more opportunities when you shift your point of view to the customer's point of view. The most common pitfall is to look at your product from only your own viewpoint and not from the customer's.

Make a list in three columns: The first column is the item you want to sell (such as music CDs), the next column describes your potential customer, and the last column is the actual product your customer buys—the benefit you are providing (entertainment, convenience, price, etc.). Remember that a customer is a person who exchanges money for your product or service. He or she is looking for reasons to buy, but at the same time he or she is looking for reasons *not* to buy. Your job in business is to turn prospects into customers by showing them a benefit appealing enough for them to part with their hard-earned money. Not everyone who breathes is a prospect—only those who have a need that you can fill are genuine prospects. Make sure that the benefits in column three are enough for the potential customer described in column two to buy your product in column one.

Prospects come in three categories—cold, warm, and hot. A "cold" prospect is someone with whom you have not yet made contact, the person driving by your location, seeing your product or company listed on an internet search engine, reading your advertising piece, and so on. Your objective is to grab their interest and get them to pick up the telephone and call, go to your website, or to stop by your location. Once you've made contact in some way, they now become a "warm" prospect. Once you establish that they have a need that you can fill, they now become a "hot" prospect. If you can show them enough benefit, they will exchange their money for your goods or services.

Depending on the nature of your business, you may already have a warm market where you have prospects. In that case, you will have to look for a connection between the person and the product you sell. Then, you truly have a warm market that you can turn into a hot market. So, if you are marketing to a particular industry or type of business, before you make the call, write the ad, create the website, design the mail piece, or any other action, ask yourself what need your product will fill. Your objective is to take that "cold" prospect, turn it into a "warm" prospect, and then into a "hot" one as soon as possible.

GETTING PAID FOR EVERYTHING YOU DO

Don't think in terms of just selling your product. Look past the initial sale—you get paid for *everything* you do for your customer and paid in much more than just dollars for the first order.

- You get paid in repeat orders when you develop a relationship with your customer.
- You get paid with purchases of other products.
- You get paid in the referrals they give you.
- You get paid in long-term customer loyalty.
- You get paid in the satisfaction of knowing you did your best to serve the customer.
- And you get paid in the added profit you make from your business as it grows.

A recent survey disclosed the six major reasons that customers switch representatives, where they shopped, or their brand of product: 68 percent switched because of negativism or indifference, 17 percent had unresolved complaints, 6 percent switched because of price, 5 percent started buying from relatives or someone they knew, 3 percent moved, and 1 percent died. Obviously, the first three, which make up 91 percent, are the ones you can have a major influence upon. Even number four—when customers get to know you as their friend and have a relationship with you, they're less likely to go anywhere else. The key is to make sure that your customers have a *joyful* experience with you, your company, your employees, your customer service, and the products you sell them. If they don't, you need to know why not, and if they are not satisfied, you need to make corrections.

If you want to develop long-term customer loyalty, the first step is to understand what you are selling. You should view your product from two points of view: the product's features (what you as the seller sees) and the product's benefits (what your customer will gain from owning or using your product). Features are what I call "head stuff," whereas benefits are "heart stuff." Plus, great customer service should be a benefit no matter what product you're selling.

For example, a few years back I purchased a new Audi. It was a very nice automobile. After driving it for about six months, I was in the Porsche-Audi dealership getting it serviced. My brother-in-law worked there as a salesman and he was one of the top Porsche salesmen in the country. While I was waiting for my car, I went into the showroom to spend some time with him. While we were talking, I noticed a new Porsche on display that was all tricked out with custom tires and wheels and other accessories, a great looking car. My first mistake was asking him about the price of the car. He said, "I don't know, let's go see." As we approached the car, he said, "Isn't this a great-looking automobile?" I said, "Yes, it is." That was my second mistake.

He opened the door, got in, and turned on the stereo. He knew I liked good music and a great sound system. Once it was cranked up, he got out and said, "Get in. You're going to love this sound system." I climbed in and sat down. That was my third mistake.

He said, "Close the door so you can get the full effect." I closed the door, and while I was sitting there, I was thinking, "I fit into this thing quite nicely." I had always thought that a Porsche was a beautiful small car, but since I am over six feet tall, I didn't think I could fit in one. But the stereo was awesome and I felt good sitting there in the car. That was my fourth mistake. I rolled down the window, and my brother-in-law backed away a couple of steps and said, "Boy, you look good in that baby!" And I said, "I do, don't I?" That was my fifth mistake.

Then he said, "Let's take this baby for a ride!" As he was rolling open the showroom doors, I remember thinking, "I'm being sold," but by that time I couldn't stop! We got into the car and off we went. That was my final mistake—driving the car. My brother-in-law knew that I liked fast cars. Before I knew what was happening, I was traveling at about 120 miles per hour on a nearly deserted freeway. That was it—I had to have that car! I went home with a brand new Porsche and my Audi never made it out of the service department.

Did I purchase the car because I needed a new one? Did I purchase it because of the features or the benefits it offered? Did I make a logical decision or an emotional decision? I bought it because I looked and felt good in that car, that's why I bought it. There was no logic in my decision. I already had a new car, but my heart and my emotions told me this one would serve me better, or at least I would look better in it!

KNOW WHY PEOPLE BUY

Let's look at some examples of selling features versus selling benefits.

You sell drill bits. Your customer is buying perfectly drilled round holes that are the same size.

You sell carpet cleaning. Your customer is buying a way to effectively remove unsightly stains from his or her carpet.

You sell dresses. Your customer is buying fashion, looking good, style.

You sell nutritional products. Your customer is buying good health, energy, feeling better, living longer.

You sell time-shares in real estate. Your customer is buying a memorable family vacation every year.

You sell new homes. Your customer is buying a dream, a place to raise the children, a tax write-off, comfort, security.

You sell food and drink in your restaurant. Your customer is buying taste, presentation, atmosphere, a great wine list, and service. I live in a small town in northern California. At a favorite restaurant called New Moon that my wife and I frequent, they serve great food, they have a great wine list, and they always provide us with great service. When we make a reservation, they always seat us at our favorite table. They had really comfortable high-backed chairs that we loved, but one evening we found that they had refurnished the restaurant with new chairs. I mentioned to the owner that we didn't like the new chairs as well as the old ones. The next time we came in for dinner, not only did they seat us at our favorite table, but there were two of the old high-back chairs at our table. That was over four years ago, and every visit since they have the chairs we love at our table. How could we not go back with that sort of service?

No matter what you are selling, people for the most part aren't that concerned about how your product works. Their biggest concern is *"Does it work?"* and, more importantly, *"Does it work for them?"* Does it fill a need *they* have and offer them a specific benefit? I don't know a thing about computers and yet I own five of them. Did I buy them because of the processor speed or the gigabytes of memory? No, all I wanted to know was whether or not it would do what *I* wanted it to do.

Will the product help your customers better their life in some way? Will it save them time or money, make them feel better, help them lose weight, and so on? Find out what your customer wants and then sell them that. If I want to purchase a black suit at your clothing store, the first thing you need to know as the salesperson is that I'm looking to buy a black suit. If you know that, there's no need to try to present me with a white one. If I don't know what color I want, it's your job to qualify me by finding out what color might work well for me.

Remember this basic rule: People are looking for reasons *to buy* your product and, on the other side of that same coin, people are also looking for reasons *not* to buy your product. Most people have a certain amount of money to spend, a budget in mind for a certain product. The question in their mind is "Does this product provide me with the benefit I'm looking for at the price I can afford?"

W.I.I.F.M.

Seeing your customer's point of view is paramount. In other words, speak their language. What does it mean to speak your customer's language? Here's what your customer wants to know before they buy:

- What will your product do for me?
- How will it solve my problem?
- How will it make my life easier?
- How will it save me money?
- W.I.I.F.M. "**W**hat's **I**n **I**t **F**or **M**e?" Why should I buy your product?

So, don't talk about features unless they want to talk about features for their benefit. Sell the features as benefits. One of the most important, and often overlooked, elements of any sales and marketing campaign is the value proposition, a statement that lets prospective customers know why they should buy from you. "Tastes great, less filling" or "Eat fresh" or "Fly the friendly skies." When you think of GEICO Insurance, you probably think, "Save up to 15 percent on your car insurance." Can you think of a better slogan about saving money, one that would have worked more effectively? Probably not, unless it was "save up to 20 percent."

Figure out what makes your product different or unique. What real-world results can prospective customers expect from your products? Will they save time or cut expenses? Improve efficiency or increase sales? Once you decide what you're offering, include the benefit in your value proposition. If you currently have customers, ask them why they buy from you. Get input from employees or friends as well. Make a list of the benefits of using your product or service. If you have more than one, take each product in your line and create a list of benefits. If you have a staff that works with you, make sure that they also understand the benefits of using your product.

Once you know the standard benefits, then you will need to customize the standard benefits to support each individual's specific needs. You do that by *learning to ask questions and listen.* If you're in a situation where you are not able to ask questions, such as marketing on the internet or by direct mail, you have to determine in advance of your marketing campaign what questions people will have about your product. Or, more importantly, what is the main selling feature of your product and what benefits are consumers looking to receive? Then, satisfy those questions within your written copy. Even organizing a focus group with potential customers might be helpful.

If you can ask questions directly, you'll want to make every effort to find out your customer's specific needs, wants, lifestyle, budget amount, color, size, and so on. For example, if someone is overweight and you want to introduce him or her to a product that will help him or her lose weight, here are some questions you could ask:

"How much weight do you want to lose?"

"Have you tried other programs? "

"How did they work for you?"

"What did you like least about the other programs?"

"What did you like most about the other programs?"

"How much money did you spend on your last program?"

"What is your budget?"

"How much do you think you've spent on weight loss programs to date?"

"What would you consider to be an ideal weight loss program?"

"What is your current plan for maintaining your weight?"

"If there was a program that was guaranteed to work, would you be interested in knowing more about it?"

You might also want to find out as much as you can about his or her lifestyle, exercise level, general state of health, and desired weight loss. Questions help your customers to further discover that they truly do have a need, and self-discovery versus telling them is more powerful. For example, you could ask someone, "How much weight do you want to lose?" or you could tell them, "You look fat and you could stand to lose some weight." Which approach do you think might get the most favorable response and build a stronger relationship? By asking questions, not only do you gather information about what's important to them, but you also help them to *discover* what they may be missing, what they truly want and need, or what they may be doing wrong.

That's also what advertising is about—you are helping them to discover that they have a problem and that you have a solution to their problem. When you ask questions to determine their needs, you can base your presentation on the *specific* benefits they would receive as a result of using your products. In other words, through questions and listening closely to your prospects' response, you can now speak *their* language. Their language revolves around the question *"How will your product benefit me?"*—and that's the only language you should use as well.

If you are marketing on the internet or where you don't have personal contact, it will be up to you to determine in general what your customers' needs might be and then satisfy their questions within your advertising copy by showing them a benefit. The first step is getting their attention, getting them to read past the first few words. You have to engage them in some way, and if you don't do it quickly, they are gone!

For example, if you go to my website www.jimbritt.com, you'll find a page designed to sell a certain program with this advertising copy:

Do you ever find yourself experiencing any of the following feelings and emotions?

- *Anxious or worried?*
- *Stressed on the job and at home?*

- *Unfulfilled relationships?*
- *Emotionally exhausted?*
- *Time pressured?*
- *Loneliness?*
- *Feeling of being out of control?*
- *Financial pressure?*
- *Depression?*
- *Impatience?*
- *Fear of the unknown?*
- *Rejected?*

We all do. In fact, we all spend a great deal of our time and energy in every area of our lives dealing with those sorts of feelings and emotions.

This opening is designed to get people engaged, to get their attention, and to get them to discover (or rediscover) that they have one or more of the above problems. Do you think that this opening would grab the attention of most people? It goes on to say the following:

Take a quick inventory of how you spend your day. If you're like most people, you'll be absolutely astounded at how much time you spend on feelings and emotions that don't get you what you want.

But maybe you already realize that you spend a lot of time on unproductive feelings. Maybe you've already tried different ways to tackle the problem. Have you . . .

- *Programmed your mind*
- *Compiled lists*
- *Attended personal growth seminars*
- *Read self-help books*
- *Participated in encounter groups*

- *Affirmed the positive*
- *Listened to subliminal tapes*
- *Sought spiritual truth at retreats*
- *Followed a guru*
- *Pulled your own strings*
- *Walked on fire*
- *and more?*

If you've read this far, the odds are you've tried one or more of the above and discovered many hours and dollars later that you're the same "old you" with maybe a few minor improvements.

Many programs promise to deliver, but few actually do. And there's a reason for this that I'll get to in just a few minutes.

But first . . . How would you like to discover the real secret to success and happiness? Imagine being able to let go of self-imposed limitations, living virtually stress-free and having peace of mind! What if you could transform your life into what you always dreamed it would be . . . A life filled with personal happiness, financial freedom, fulfilling relationships, vibrant health, and more!

That's just one example of engaging your prospect by showing potential benefit. The key is to grab the person's attention and get him or her to read further. You ask questions that you know people will answer "yes" to in their mind as they read.

DISCOVER WHAT OTHERS WANT

Instead of thinking about what you are selling, learn to think in terms of "what the customer wants." What will trigger them to buy or want to know more? Keep in mind that your prospects have four basic questions that need to be satisfied, questions that they may or may not ask you outright but they'll certainly have them in their minds.

What is it? What are you selling? This will account for 10 percent of your presentation's result.

How does it work? The simple basics of what you are selling. This will account for about 10 percent of the effectiveness of your presentation.

How much does it cost? This, too, accounts for about 10 percent of the effectiveness of your presentation.

How will it help me? The benefit will account for about 70 percent of the effectiveness of your presentation.

Therefore, if you don't create specific benefits that support your customers' needs, you'll only have a 30 percent chance of making the sale. On the other hand, you may be in a highly competitive field where people are shopping for price. In that case, you may use price as a benefit, or you might stress faster delivery, better service, and so on.

My brother-in-law, the one that sold me the Porsche, started selling BMWs. He told me about a wealthy gentleman who came in to purchase a $120,000 BMW. Just as the man signed the check, he looked over and said, "You know, young man, I could go down the street to another dealer and purchase this car for thousands less, but you did such a masterful presentation and I really liked your style that I consider it a pleasure buying from you." By the way, I now drive a BMW!

Focus most of your efforts on "how it will help," even if you leave out all the rest. In fact, if a potential customer sees a strong enough benefit, none of the rest will matter much at all.

Another winning combination is to "under-promise" and "over-deliver." Look for ways to consistently surpass your customer's expectations:

Don't set the bar too low. In other words, don't set the target too low just to guarantee success. This approach may lessen the value of your product in your customer's eyes. Set a realistic goal that's attainable.

Don't set the bar too high. Often, you get caught up in the excitement of making the sale and promise more than can realistically be delivered. This sets you up to fail. Over-promising can also cause undue pressure, burnout, missed deadlines, lost opportunities, and, of course, lost future business.

Know your limitations. Figure out how long it will realistically take to fill an order and base your promises on that, allowing yourself time for unforeseen delays.

Keep striving to improve. Make improved efficiency a team effort and objective. Look for ways to save time by reducing unnecessary steps, without compromising quality.

RELATIONSHIP NETWORKING

Although it may not always be appropriate or you may not have a face-to-face relationship with your customer, whenever possible ask for referrals, whether or not a customer buys. I call it developing a "relationship network." Some of your best referrals may even come from those who didn't buy from you. And if you aren't actually doing any face-to-face selling in your business (marketing on the internet or using direct mail), it would serve you well to implement some sort of referral program. For instance, some websites offer an affiliate program, which compensates the people for anyone they refer who makes a purchase.

How do you get a referral? First of all, you have to ask. Create a program to encourage prospects or customers to offer referrals. Second, you have to deserve it: If your customer or prospect is satisfied that you did a good job or that you have a superior product, and he or she trusts that you will treat his or her friend or business associate fairly, he or she will give you referrals. Keep in mind that everyone knows someone who could use your product. That's how books and movies are sold and that's how people find out about great restaurants.

Do not assume that your product will provide a benefit for everyone, because it won't. But every person who says "no" has friends or business associates who may say "yes." Granted, you won't sell a weight loss program to a skinny person, but rest assured that every skinny person knows numerous people who need to lose weight. In fact, when you look at diet drink marketing, they use skinny people to advertise. They market to everyone—overweight people want to get skinny and skinny people want to stay that way!

Here are some quick tips for sharing information about your products with prospective customers:

- Always be considerate of your customer's time.

- Always ask for permission to show or demonstrate your products.

- Always ask for referrals and offer some kind of incentive, if you can.

- Have something specific you want to say to your prospect and practice it until it becomes natural.

- Decide what sales materials and methods you will use to present your product, and be ready at all times.

- Listen for clues, desires, needs, problems, etc., in what your customer says.

- Talk about benefits, not features. Benefits show *what your product will do for them.*

- Ask questions about how they might utilize your product, and listen.

- Always tell the truth and be concise.

- Don't make any exaggerated claims or false representations about your product.

Also, build a relationship with your customer. Here are some ways of doing that:

- Pass on new product information regularly to old customers.

- Obtain their street or e-mail address and, if possible, send them a thank you note or announcements of special sales or new merchandise. If appropriate, keep records of your customer's birthdays or other special occasions and send them a card.

- If you operate from a retail location, greet every customer with "hello" when they enter, and go the extra mile and say "goodbye" when they leave as well. Saying "hello" is common, but saying "goodbye" requires a little more caring. In fact, people may remember you more for your "goodbye."

- Attempt to establish a first-name basis to the relationship. A person's name is a sweet sound to his or her ears, and if you say "thank you" along with his or her name, that's even better. If the person is a regular customer, greeting him or her by his or her first name will go a long way toward developing a long-term relationship.

- Listen and communicate clearly. Good communication skills will help to eliminate problems that may damage relationships.

- Keep your place of business clean and conducive to doing business.

- If you are in a situation where you have set appointments, be prompt. Being late is rude and unprofessional. It shows a lack of self-discipline and a lack of respect for your client's time.

THINK "SUCCESS"

Think "success" and be positive. Life seems to have a way of becoming a self-fulfilling prophecy, so think about success and act as if failure is not an option. When you think "success," you will attract customers who will support you in your endeavor. Besides, it takes a lot less energy to think "success" rather than worrying about failure.

Give compliments. Compliments start with feeling good about yourself. If you feel good about yourself, you are more likely to see reasons to compliment others. The bottom line is to make sure that your customers have a joyful experience with you—with their experience at your location, on your website, with customer service, with your company, with your product, with your delivery time, and with your follow-up—and you will have them for life.

To summarize this chapter, remember these points:

- What are you selling? What is your product?

- Who are your customers? Who is your target market?

- How do you expose your product to that market—what marketing methods will you utilize?

- How will your product benefit your customer? What are you really selling?

- Develop a strategic plan and understand that plans can change and will need refining as you go. The key is to just get started.

- Stay focused on the end result.

- Start small, but think big and reach for the top!

- Learn from the best in your chosen industry.

- Learn the skill of selling and making the deal.

- Develop long-term relationships with your customers.

- And last, but most important, learn selling. The most important part of selling is learning why people buy, not simply learning the skill of selling. Selling begins and ends with building long-term relationships with value for both parties involved. The difference between success and mediocrity in sales is your philosophy—adopt a philosophy that drives you to a higher standard, one that is driven by values and centers on helping.

A basic fundamental of success is having passion about what you sell. If you're not on fire about it, you're going to lose the sale to someone else who is!

10

Develop Your Leadership Skills

If you thought you could truly make a difference, would you be willing to step out of the crowd and be all that you can be? If you discovered that you possessed untapped leadership qualities and skills, would you use them? If you knew that you could inspire others to greater levels of achievement, to make a significant difference in their lives, would you feel compelled to do so? No matter what your current role may be or what business you are in, you should consider choosing to become a more powerful, effective leader. With a few simple, yet powerful, tools, you can develop your leadership skills and use them to become more influential, more effective in dealing with others, and more inspiring to others to perform at their optimum level.

There are men and women just like you, from all sorts of businesses and from every social and economic level, making a difference because they have developed their leadership skills and put them into action. They, like you, care deeply about something, and they want to use their skills to become more powerful and influential. They use their leadership skills to make a difference and they become different themselves.

What sets effective leaders apart? It's not their level of education or how much money they earn. It's not where they come from or who they know. It's not their sex, age, or occupation. What sets them apart is their awareness and sensitivity to the needs of others, an awareness of the challenges people face and how to make a contribution or provide a solution. It's also their enthusiasm for improving things and for creating new opportunities. They have a passion for a cause bigger than themselves, and they have a deep desire to give something back to society. And in looking for ways to make a difference and serve others, they tap their hidden abilities, unleash their authentic power, and fully develop their leadership potential.

THE QUALITIES OF A GREAT LEADER

There are common qualities that effective leaders possess, characteristics inherent in all of us when we put forth the effort to recognize and develop them. To develop them, you are not required to study complex theories or perform psychological gymnastics. These are common-sense ideas and attitudes that individually and collectively can make you a more dynamic, effective leader. Some of these qualities are "how to" skills and some are "people" skills, while others may involve philosophy, psychology, and attitude.

Leadership is not something you learn once and for all and you're done. It is an ever-evolving set of skills, ideas, and talents that evolve and change as you do. To become an effective leader, you must have a clear definition of what leadership qualities are, a willingness to improve yourself, and a desire to make a difference in the lives of others. True leadership is the art of inspiring others to action through one's own exemplary behavior. You become a mentor through your own actions and your very presence. Effective leaders inspire others to aim higher, to work harder and smarter, to accomplish more in less time, and to enjoy doing it. The following are qualities of a great leader.

- You inspire your team with a vision of success.
- You are sensitive to every individual's needs.
- You challenge your team to stay focused and on purpose.

- You encourage and support your team when they are down.
- You keep your team motivated and focused on winning.
- You are a mentor for your team, by setting an example and by sharing your insights and experiences.
- You provide the common vision and mission that holds the team together.
- You inspire your team to give their best despite the odds.
- And you encourage your team to take the initiative, to work together, and to make contributions that benefit the organization as a whole.

Leadership simply means the courage to be first. Leadership is action, not a position you attain. In most sports, without a coach or leader, the player wouldn't know how to score, which direction to run, or maybe not even how to play the game at all. Everyone needs a coach, someone to teach him or her the rules of the game and keep him or her focused on winning. Otherwise, a person might spend all of his or her time on the defensive, not knowing that the only way to win is playing the offensive. Each member of your team is special and wants to feel good about himself or herself as well as about being a part of a unique team—that's your job. The attitude and performance of your team will determine the success of your business.

As a leader, the following are a few simple principles that you may find serve you well in keeping your team members performing at their peak.

A Great Leader Has a Vision

Vision is defined as "seeing with your imagination." As a leader, it's important to clearly know where you are going and, even more importantly, why—why do you want what you want? What compels you to do what you do? What's the passion behind your vision?

You'll discover the answer to your compelling "why" when you find the true purpose that drives you, the pure essence of what you want. You want to build a successful company? Why? You want to become financially free? Why? What does being financially free mean to you?

Your vision can be small or earthshaking, but it must be clear. This means knowing both what you want to accomplish and why you want to accomplish it. Your vision as a leader, whether *clear* or *fuzzy,* will have an effect on those around you. Your clarity as well as your commitment to your vision becomes an example to inspire and motivate others to clarify their own vision and become a part of the whole. Your clear vision will become the powerful magnetic quality that is at the heart of effective leadership and at the heart of every successful company.

A Great Leader Is an Example

As a leader, you live under a microscope—nothing you do or say escapes the scrutiny and examination of your followers. That microscope is one of the most important secrets of effective leadership, because your followers mirror the example you set for them. As a leader, ask yourself repeatedly, "What message am I sending?" "What example am I setting?" and "What environment am I creating?" When you as a leader set out to make a difference in your company, your beliefs, your words, and your actions inspire others to follow you. As a leader, setting the example comes first and foremost because you are accountable to your team and for the success of your company.

Never ask your team members to do, or expect them to do, something that you wouldn't do yourself. Remember, leadership is action, not position. Being a leader is not something you are given, it's who you are. Leadership determines how you show up, how you appear to your followers, and what message you send to your team to follow. If you as a leader don't return phone calls, for example, you are teaching your team members not to follow-up. You must "talk the talk" and "walk the walk," if you want others to follow your lead.

A Great Leader Serves Others

Serving others has a high value. In fact, the word *president* is defined as "master servant." If you contribute your time, energy, emotions, and effort, you will have a real impact on your team members and their performance. When you make a contribution to the well-being and performance of others, your level of success will increase.

Service is an attitude, not a department. Everyone within an organization needs to be responsible for service. Your willingness and ability to serve others, how deep your service runs, and the type, kind, and quality of service given will be major keys to your success and the success of the organization. Effective leaders know that service starts at the top—your slogan as leader should be "Service starts here."

A Great Leader Is Responsible for Everything

A leader's job is influencing human behavior, regardless of the goal. They never point toward someone else or an outside circumstance as the cause of their problems. They take full responsibility for their own actions, the actions of their team, as well as the end result produced. If there's a problem, they simply get it fixed.

I knew a man who said that he always attracted people who would not respect his "demands." No matter who he hired, they always eventually turned out the same way—they just were not supportive of his demands. After some further conversation, I asked him if he wanted to hear the unvarnished truth, and he did.

"First, you can't 'demand' respect and support from your team, you have to earn it. They have to be inspired to support you," I said. "Second, you are the problem, not them. You can't control the actions and attitudes of your people, but you can control yourself. When you take the responsibility to change yourself, others around you will change. You'll begin to attract more supportive people."

Taking responsibility for your own behaviors is the key to getting your team to respond favorably to your lead. Responsibility simply means "the ability to respond." If you don't take responsibility, you have no ability to respond. A leader takes full responsibility for how he or she feels, for his or her own behaviors, and for the behavior and results of the entire team.

A great leader also knows that team building is like a farmer planting a crop. The farmer plants seeds and each seed is unique—some will grow and some won't; it's the law of averages. If the farmer wants to improve his average and increase his yield, he simply increases the nourishment, and that's always a fine balance. He has to take care to keep the weeds out so they don't choke his crop. He can provide too much or too little nourishment, and either one can destroy the crop. It's your job as a leader to nourish your team and to keep the weeds out. You have to be quick with the hoe to cut the weeds of fear, doubt, bad attitude, conflict, or other types of negativity that will smother your harvest. As a leader, you must take full responsibility for the growth and yield of your team, whether your team is one person or five hundred.

A Great Leader Challenges Each Team Member to Become More

Help each individual team member to see more in himself or herself, to further develop toward becoming a more valuable team member. If you help people grow as individuals, they will stay with you. Challenge them to earn more, to grow more, to stretch, to learn, and to apply that learning. Encourage them to get involved in decision-making in their area of expertise. Challenge them to let go of their fears and to take on more responsibility.

Help your team members get what they want, even if it is just knowing that they will get a paycheck on time. The higher up the ladder in management and the higher their income, the more they will need to see a brighter future for themselves. If you don't show them where they can advance to, they will eventually take their talents and market them elsewhere, which can be very costly to you. Find out what they want out of life and then help them get it.

A Great Leader Keeps People Connected

The greatest of all human needs is the need to feel connected. This "heart connection" is what I call "nutrition for the soul" and people in organizations all over the world are dying from malnutrition of the soul. They are dying because they have lost that sense of connection. Your team members need to feel connected and valued for the part they play on the team. What should you do to keep your people connected?

Keep them connected to you. The more you care for others, the more they feel connected and committed to you. Keep them connected to you by becoming their mentor for success.

Keep them connected to their goals and dreams. Never let them lose sight of the person they want to become.

Keep them connected to your products and services. Remind them often of the benefits and the quality of your products or services as well as the benefit for others.

Keep them connected to the team. Your team can become like a family. People love being a part of something larger than themselves.

Keep them connected to the company. Help them to see the company as their partner in business and to see themselves as an integral part of that partnership.

Keep them connected to the cause. The cause is what the whole team is working toward achieving—the company's mission and vision, or helping others to improve their quality of life, or what your product does for the end user. Whatever it is, keep them connected to something that is much greater than money.

Every time you have contact with a team member, ask yourself, "How can I reconnect with them? What does he or she need today that would help maintain the connection?" If every person on your team was connected in every way, how would he or she feel? How would he or she perform? How dedicated would he or she be?

A Great Leader Cares for the Team

What if you owned a goose that laid golden eggs? Every morning when you awoke, there would be a new fourteen-carat, solid gold goose egg. How would you care for your goose? Would you feed it well and give it the finest grain and the healthiest food you could find? Would you keep it warm at night and tuck it into bed . . . and *not* use a down-filled comforter? If you had a goose that laid golden eggs, you would take *very* good care of it.

But if you chased the goose to try to make it lay the golden eggs—that's the approach most people take—you'd end up with a handful of feathers on pay day and that's about it! If you care for your goose, build a relationship with it so that it doesn't fly south and never return, you'll end up with a fortune. Your goose is your team.

A flock of geese fly in formation together as a team and there's always a head goose in the formation. That's you as the leader. You will also hear the flying geese "honking." If you peered through a telescope and observed the flock in flight, the first thing you'll notice is that the leader is not honking. The leader is working hard. The rest of the flock is not honking either, but rather cheering the leader on, saying, in effect, "Go! Go! Go! Go!" You may also notice that the leader doesn't remain a leader for long—the geese all take turns being the leader. When one leader tires, he then drops back in the middle of the formation and rests while another takes over. Did you know that on a long flight, a flock of geese fly 72 percent faster than an individual goose flies alone? Isn't teamwork amazing?

The same holds true with leadership. You can fly much faster and accomplish more by working together as a team. And you can accomplish much more by letting others take over and be leaders in their area of expertise. Care for your team. Be accountable for your team and, at the same, time teach others to be accountable for themselves and for the team. Remember, personal accountability is where your success begins. Develop an attitude that, as a leader, you are an integral part of every event and every person's life, as well as the success of the business.

As a leader, it's not what happens that's important, it's how you respond to what happens that makes all the difference in the world. Making connections builds an emotional bond, emotional bonds create relationships, and building relationships is what being an effective leader is all about.

A Great Leader Appreciates Every Team Member

Take every opportunity to show appreciation for each team member and the effort he or she makes. Everyone wants to be appreciated—the person answering the telephone, the field sales representative, the office manager, the janitor, and so on. Let no one go unnoticed or unrecognized—let them know how much you appreciate their help, dedication, and performance. If you have someone who is always working late or coming in early just to get the job done, going the extra mile and making a significant contribution, let him or her know that you appreciate the extra effort.

Whenever possible, recognition should occur in front of other team members. Send a note, take the person to lunch, or give them an award. There's always something to be appreciated in every person. Let it be known and don't keep it a secret. Remember to recognize them for little successes. Praise for your team members should be a part of your philosophy of managing people. Always be quick to give praise, because it makes people feel special and their commitment to the team, to you, and to their performance will increase as a result. You don't have to wait for great successes or a record-breaking month to give praise—constantly look for ways to offer recognition.

A Great Leader Is a Good Listener

The most successful leaders are those who have developed the ability to listen to their people. As your organization grows, people will always have things that bother them and that they need to express. By listening, you achieve several things: You develop an emotional bond with them for caring and listening, you help them get their problem solved or off their mind, and you help them to be a productive team member once again.

Remember, when someone has a problem that doesn't get

solved, he or she is not as productive as could be. You also run the risk of the problem affecting the attitude and performance of the entire team. Because if you, as their team leader, don't listen, they will go to their peers to discuss their problems. One of the fastest ways to destroy an organization's morale is the coffee room rehashing of problems. Problem-solving communication should come from the top down, not the bottom up.

A Great Leader Studies Human Nature on Three Levels

Leaders study *possibility.* What *could* exist? Leaders understand that there is always something more that they could do to benefit the team as a whole. They look for ways to assist each member's personal growth. They are constantly playing the "what if" game with themselves as well as each member of the team.

Leaders study *opportunity.* They know that every encounter with another presents an opportunity to make a connection, to further develop a relationship, and to improve performance. They are always looking for ways to connect in order to better themselves, the company, and every team member. Every meeting they conduct, every e-mail they send out, and every telephone call they make represents an opportunity to develop a relationship and improve the individual's performance.

Leaders study *inevitability.* If you were to start driving your car on Interstate 10 in Jacksonville, Florida, and you headed west, where would you end up if you didn't stop? You would inevitably run off the end of the Santa Monica Pier in southern California. A great leader watches the direction where each member of his or her team is headed, and knows inevitably where they are going to end up on their present course. He or she also knows when to make course corrections and helps others to see the corrections they need to make.

There's a story about an egotistical captain of a battleship. One night, he was navigating in heavy fog. Suddenly, he saw a blinking light dead ahead. He radioed with a message, "We are on a collision course, change your course 30 degrees to the left." A message came back, "You change your course 30 degrees to the left."

Feeling a little put out, he radioed again, "I am a captain, change your course 30 degrees to the left." The message came back, "I am also a captain, change your course 30 degrees to the left."

Getting angry, he radioed back, "I am a battleship and I suggest you change your course 30 degrees to the left!" The message came back, "I am a lighthouse, and I suggest you change your course 30 degrees to the left."

As you move forward, you will almost certainly encounter obstacles. A good leader looks ahead and knows what he or she is dealing with, then takes immediate, appropriate action to solve the problem with the least amount of conflict. Also, know that strength cannot exist without resistance. A good leader always looks for the point of strength in every obstacle encountered. The limit of the current view does not represent his or her capacity to create a solution to a problem.

A Great Leader Is Resourceful

A leader knows that every action he or she takes is either *resourceful,* moving him or her closer to his desired objective, or it is *nonresourceful,* moving him or her away from his or her objective. What is necessary is the wisdom to know the difference. Resourceful leaders manage their actions more than anything else. They continually ask themselves, "Is this action I'm taking moving me closer to or further from my desired result? Is it resourceful or nonresourceful?" If it is not taking either the leader or the team in the appropriate direction, they quickly choose another course of action.

A Great Leader Is Sensitive

Sensitive leadership is not leadership that lacks strength or courage. Being sensitive does not lessen a leader's power, as some might think. A sensitive leader has a heightened awareness of his or her issues and values as well as those of the people within his or her organization. To be a sensitive leader simply means that you have the ability to stay focused on the world in which you operate and on the people you lead.

Sensitivity doesn't distract from other leadership qualities, rather it adds to them. For example, decision-making requires a greater sensitivity because, as an entrepreneur, you're in a business that can change rapidly. That makes it a risky business, and risk requires being sensitive to all the elements of the risk, including the potential outcomes for all involved. Risk-taking is a major part of leadership. When you consider successful leaders who make a difference, you see that they have the courage to take action, while others wait for a better time, a safer situation, or assured results. They are decisive and move forward, because they know that being too cautious and indecisive kills opportunity.

A sensitive leader is a good listener and takes input from team members. He or she knows that if a team member has doubts and feels that he or she should not express them, the doubt can lead to uncertainty and lack of clarity, which may negatively impact productivity. They also know that doubt in one team member may transfer to others. Being sensitive to the needs of your people is crucial to your leadership effectiveness, because without responsive, productive people, all the other considerations quickly become secondary.

A Great Leader Manages Planning and Activity, Not Results

The result already produced is a past issue. You can't manage results, but you can manage activity. Activity is what the team members have the potential to produce. So, focus your effort where it counts—on planning, strategizing, and productive activities.

A Great Leader Doesn't Have an Ego

Don't let success go to your head. Don't get caught up in your own ego and forget the very qualities that earned you success in the first place. Remember that you are in a "people and relationship business," and the day you forget that is the day you will have to start over. Successful people are secure and self-confident—they know who they are, where their talents lie, and their limitations. They don't have to make themselves look bigger or make others look smaller in order to feel successful. Truly successful people view their responsibilities as a leader, the demands on their time, and their level of success with humility.

BRING OUT THE BEST

In any business, people are your most valuable resource. Inspiring them to give their best efforts will be a major key to your long-term success. Every coach has a game plan, every military officer has a battle plan, every airline pilot has a flight plan, every teacher has a lesson plan, and every leader should have a plan for bringing out the best in him- or herself and others. When you and your company eventually end up in the winner's circle, you can rest assured that it wasn't by accident—it was because you and your team collectively did your jobs, and because you, as the team leader, did your job very well.

11

The Power of Letting Go

In every book I write and every time I address a group, I always feel compelled to cover one of my favorite subjects—the power of "letting go." Have you ever experienced anxiety, worry, fear, stress about lack of time, financial pressure, insecurity about your future, or impatience? I'm sure we all have. In fact, most of us spend a great deal of our time and energy trying to overcome these feelings and emotions. Many years ago, I began to see the obvious: That the underlying cause of most people's problems, unhappiness, and lack of success (including my own) was not the lack of new motivating ideas to change external conditions but rather our disempowering beliefs, feelings, and behaviors. Letting go deals with the causes rather than the effects.

LOOK FOR A SOLUTION

If you are driving down the highway at 70 miles an hour and the bridge is out ahead, you don't speed up! You slow down to look for an alternate route. If you have a problem, you don't speed up and ignore it. You slow down and look for a solution.

Let's say you are in sales and you want to make more sales but have a fear of talking to people. That's a problem. To overcome it, you don't blindly go forward hoping the fear will go away. The solution is to learn to deal with and let go of your fear, to deal with the root cause of your problem. If you want more happiness, you learn to let go of the things that are causing your unhappiness, instead of trying to ignore your unhappiness and hoping that will bring you more happiness. If you want more success, letting go of the disempowering feelings, emotions, and behaviors that are blocking your success is the answer. Take action, but first let go of things that throw you off track.

Remember this simple success tool that I've mentioned several times before: Every action you take is either moving you toward what you want or further away from it. Success in anything is that simple. A fear is either taking you closer to or further away from what you really want in your life. If it's taking you in the wrong direction, recognizing it is the first step, and the second step is dealing with it.

LETTING GO IS SIMPLE AND NATURAL

Letting go is simple and easy to understand. There is no system to follow or exercises to do while lying on the floor. Every time you make a decision, you let go of the alternate one. Should I take this direction or that one? The question is, are you letting go of the right one? Are you honoring what will move you toward success or away from it?

For example, let's look at anxiety. With anxiety, you are pulled in two directions at the same time. It's like driving your car with one foot on the brake and the other on the gas pedal, wondering why you're not getting anywhere! You get inspired with your goals and plans, which will move you forward, but then like a thief in the night your old anxieties sneak in and take over, pulling you back again. No amount of external stimulation can cure an internal condition like anxiety. Speeding up is not a cure for anxiety, it's a cause—it may offer some temporary relief, but it won't and can't relieve anxiety. The greatest thief of our time, success, productivity, and happiness is anxiety produced by non-supportive feelings, beliefs, and behaviors, and we all suffer from it, to one degree or another.

The way to free yourself of anxiety is to let it go. Stop and take a look at the actions you are taking. Are they moving you in the direction you want to go or not? If not, take a different course of action. An action can be a thought, feeling, belief, or behavior. Anxiety stems from the "need to control" your circumstances. Instead of speeding up, trying to do more to relieve your anxiety, try stopping all action for a few moments—take a short walk, take a few deep breaths, close your eyes for five minutes, and watch your anxiety lessen. When you learn to let go of the need to control anxiety, you gain complete control of the present moment where the action takes place and where life takes place. With that, you gain complete control over your life and your success.

Letting go requires three things: intention, willingness, and commitment. Letting go is as simple as recognizing that you are hanging on to something that is holding you back and then choosing to take an alternate route. In my program "The Power of Letting Go," I provide a simple step-by-step process that shows you how to break free of those bad habits, unwanted feelings, and behaviors—and you'll see results the very first day you use the program.

Let's say that you are faced with a difficult situation at the office—you need to confront someone about a sensitive issue. You feel nervous, worried, and a bit fearful because you don't want to hurt the other person's feelings. First, realize that worrying about something over which you have no control is a waste of time and energy. Second, observe your feelings about the situation and ask yourself if having those feelings will move you in the direction you want to go. Third, let go of your need to control an outcome over which you have no control. Take a few deep breaths to clear yourself of that feeling and then take action without any thought of how it's going to turn out. Simply let the outcome be the outcome.

Another example: You find yourself in the middle of an argument, and anger from both sides is surfacing. Ask yourself, "Who wins in an argument?" Of course, the answer is no one! Next, observe yourself feeling angry—notice where you feel it in your body. As you observe yourself being angry, it starts to go away. And as you let go of your anger, notice how the other person changes as well. Remember, it takes two to have an argument and when you refuse to argue, the other person has no opponent and changes their approach. When you let go of the need to control, you gain complete control.

On the other hand, let's say that you are raising capital for your new business venture and find yourself feeling a need for approval from your investor. Take a deep breath and let go of your fear, and your need for approval, and allow the outcome to fall where it may. Remember, when you need approval, you get none.

Self-observation is the key element in the process of letting go. When you observe yourself with anything other than a feeling that will move you in the direction you want to go, observe the feeling and watch it begin to go away. Self-observation *is* letting go. Taking a deep breath *is* letting go. Walking away *is* letting go. Deciding not to think in a certain way *is* letting go. Challenging an old belief *is* letting go. Taking another course of action *is* letting go.

You can spend your whole life trying to change others or wishing something was different in your life, and you can spend a lifetime wishing for a different past or a better present. But you can't change others and you can't change the past. You *can* change yourself and your present condition at some point in the future by the actions you take today. It really takes no effort at all to let go. It's simple and natural, like trees shedding their leaves in the fall—they drop what they no longer need in order to make room for the new in the spring. You, too, can "make room" in your life by letting go—I've seen thousands of individuals simply and naturally create incredible changes in their lives.

LETTING GO WORKS

When something works, it works, and learning to let go really works! Let go of what's not working or what didn't work in the past, and let go of your anxiety about the future and about success. Letting go will give you the power to live your life exactly the way you choose. It will help you to look at every situation from a new point of view and to solve problems as they come up, with less tension and stress. Letting go is a powerful, life-changing process that works for everyone, a tool that you'll use for a lifetime.

12

The Beginning

Perhaps you are wondering at this point if you can really become a successful entrepreneur. Or you may be wondering how long it will take. The answer to the first question is "Yes, you can!" As for how long it will take you, that depends on you. If you have a laser focus on your objective and stay out of the pitfalls and emotional misjudgments, you'll move with great speed, especially compared to the outdated pattern of trading time for money.

You can start by not limiting your vision to what you "need" and instead focus on what you "want." Stop trying harder; rather, do something differently, which is the only way to achieve a different result. Believe only in "testing" your limits, not "in" your limits. Have faith, but not in the familiar. And stop thinking you have to do it all yourself. Don't get bogged down in preparation or wait for perfect timing. Once you find your opportunity, move on it. And if it feels comfortable to you, you aren't advancing. Advancing is going to cause you discomfort, but stepping out of your comfort zone is the only way to grow.

YOU ARE MORE THAN YOUR CURRENT STORY

For every person, the beginning is always where success starts. Our "story" is either what we tell ourselves about who we are or it's what we believe about ourselves and our abilities. If you want more of anything in your life—success, money, happiness, anything at all—then you must leave your current story behind and start a new one. Begin at the beginning, which is right now. As simplistic as that may seem, it can be tremendously empowering to understand that you can reinvent your story completely.

You must develop an intimate consciousness of being right here, right now. Otherwise, everything you attempt will inevitably become an act of self-avoidance, based on the person you used to be. Self-avoidance means you are honoring your fear and trying to escape reality—to escape what's really happening right now, to escape getting started, to escape taking responsibility or stepping out of your comfort zone. When you attempt to escape the moment to avoid handling a problem, facing a challenge, or facing something that may be painful, you take yourself out of a resourceful state and into some psychological time and space warp, into fear mode where no answers exist. You take yourself out of life, out of where the action is, which is right here, right now. How can you possibly trust yourself and be productive at anything if you turn away from yourself and try to escape reality? You can't.

At one point in my career as an entrepreneur, I began to doubt my own commitment to being effective. I would constantly berate myself for not being as good as I could be. I thought that maybe I needed more information, so I read more books and studied harder. I thought that I needed more personal growth and better communication skills, so I worked harder on myself. My desire for success, my relentless pursuit to become better, and my unwillingness to give up has played a big part in taking me where I am today.

One day, I began to look at myself and realized the amount of time and effort that I had put into becoming a whole and effective human being. If I had observed anyone else doing that amount of work on themselves, I would have marveled at their dedication, discipline, and commitment. I realized that day that I had all I needed to be successful and I decided to start giving myself the encouragment and the recognition I deserved and to stop looking elsewhere to keep myself "motivated." I also decided to stop holding back and to start taking advantage of every opportunity that came my way which supported my vision. The very next day, I was presented with the opportunity to meet the man who gave me the missing piece of the puzzle that launched my career.

WHAT MAKES A GREAT OPPORTUNITY

What opportunities should you look for? That varies with each individual and circumstance, and what makes an opportunity for you may not be one for another. An opportunity may be as simple as a perfectly timed telephone call or meeting someone with certain talents and abilities from whom you could learn. If you wanted to start a certain type of business, wouldn't it be a great opportunity to meet someone who has already made it to the top in that field? An opportunity may present itself in a multitude of ways, and sometimes more than one at a time.

Maybe you've found your perfect opportunity, and maybe not, but you now have all the tools you need to get started and be successful in a business of your own. Now, all you need is to select the right opportunity and have the courage and determination to use the tools. That courage and determination, that success mind-set, has to come from you. If you aspire to achieve great things in your business and in your life, you must be willing to put forth some serious effort. You must make success an imperative, a priority, and never forget the law of cause and effect—those who do the work, earn the pay, and those who seek are the ones who find opportunities.

Don't get bogged down in getting ready. You can make a career out of "laying the groundwork" for the big launch, but that doesn't pay very well. If doing some groundwork is part of the plan, just do it. But if you spend all your time getting ready, you may miss the opportunity altogether. Forget preparation—just get started and then make adjustments as you go. A person can spend so much time getting ready, making sure they get it right, that they never get it right and they never get started. Realize that a perfect plan before you begin will get you nowhere as an entrepreneur, because it's likely going to change once you get started anyway. So, get started and let the plan unfold.

First you act, then you work out the details of your strategy. You must take action, move on your dream, and then let what happens help you to develop a more detailed plan. Action is the crucial element. A plan will evolve out of your action. You'll soon discover that you know a lot more than you thought you knew, so trust your intuition. You are ready to take a giant step forward. All you have to do is to take the step and trust the process of discovery, and trust yourself. You will not leap forward so much as to exceed your grasp. Success is yours for the taking, right here, right now. Step forward without worrying where your foot is going to land, and then be open to utilizing the resources that you discover.

Painstaking preparation is nothing more than an excuse to hide your fear of taking the first step, a stalling tactic or an act of anxiety. It is really a con game, with yourself as the victim. You are ready right now to move to a higher level of performance, if you are willing to take the first step. Are you ready?

DO NOT PROCRASTINATE

It's all up to you—do not procrastinate or put off the application of these principles for success. They worked for me, they have worked for thousands of others, and they will work for you. Don't you feel that it's your turn to succeed, to be in the top 5 percent, financially free? Don't you feel it's your turn to have the personal freedom you've always dreamed of having?

Why shouldn't you be getting up in the morning joyful, excited about the prospective events of the day, looking forward to working for yourself and for your dreams, instead of being a player in someone else's game?

Why shouldn't you be owning your own business and being your own boss?

Why not create for yourself and your family a brand new life without limits?

Why not have your dreams come alive in the present and not in some distant future? Why wait another day? You've got the knowledge. All you have to do now is to invest the time and put forth the effort.

Why not take advantage of the free enterprise system? The more enterprising you become, the freer you become! It's not what happens to you that controls the quality of your life, it's what you *do* about what happens that counts.

Why not live your dream, and why not now? If not now, when? Don't wait another day to start creating your success story and living your dream.

SUCCESS IS RESERVED FOR THE TALENTED AND GIFTED

How about you—do you have what it takes to be successful? Are you talented or gifted? Are you willing to put yourself in a position where luck shows up on your doorstep? Whether you realize it or not, you have many gifts and talents you've never used. We all know people that we consider "gifted," who seem to be different in some way. We all know people that have earned a lot of money, perhaps through luck, but luck is simply being in the right place at the right time. We all know people who seem to stand out in the crowd in some way. The only real difference in those high achievers is that they have accepted and utilized their gifts. They seem to have more gifts than others, more talent than others, or more luck than others, but they really don't—all they did was to claim their gifts, use their talents, and accept that luck was something they created for themselves.

Right now is the time for you to begin to recognize and use your gifts. Stake your claim to them. Know that you have many gifts yet to be discovered, and when you do discover them, they will show up on your doorstep and you must reach for them. When you utilize them, they will serve you well.

Take a moment and look back in your life. Look at the skills you have developed over the years and the talents you have utilized to get you where you are today. You will discover that they are simply the gifts that you have opened. The question is, how many other gifts are within your reach? For every one that you have opened, there are hundreds more that await your unveiling. Your hidden, unused potential—your unopened gifts—are just waiting to play a major role in your next moves up the ladder of success.

Conclusion

Over the years, I have met thousands of people who think they are not very special or don't have what it takes to be rich. They think they are not smart enough, not educated enough, not experienced enough, or that they don't have enough money to get started. Their self-confidence has been suppressed and they feel unimportant, even lost. They don't believe that they have what it takes to become wealthy. Well, I believe that hidden inside each individual is a unique gift, a talent or passion, that can move mountains when awakened. I have always wanted to help people discover their unique talents and abilities and to enjoy the success they deserve. I have tried my best in this book to help you see your own uniqueness—how much you have to offer to the world, how many opportunities are available for the taking, and how to take action to make your dreams come true.

The peregrine falcon is the world's fastest animal, reported to reach speeds of up to two hundred miles per hour during vertical dives. Like the peregrine falcon, every individual is also capable of great things, at great speeds, yet they are too often restrained by an invisible leash they have created in their minds. This invisible leash limits how far and how fast they can fly. The leash is their self-imposed limitations held deep inside, woven together by poor decisions based on false beliefs. And until they are unleashed by a new decision for a new direction, they will continue to fly at their current, slow speed.

Regardless of your background or past experience, you can have anything your heart desires. The big question is, "What does your heart desire?" Start now—draw your dreams from your heart, the ones that seem just out of your reach, and decide *now* to make them a reality!

And as you move toward those dreams, remember that your greatest lessons, your greatest growth opportunities, will be disguised as obstacles. Embrace them and know that each obstacle you overcome is moving you one step closer to your desired outcome. Every time you feel discomfort, just know that it is a necessary part of the process toward success. Personal growth is uncomfortable. If you are not experiencing discomfort, you are not growing and the best part of you remains asleep! Obstacles provide you with intellectual, spiritual, and emotional stimulation so you can thrive and grow.

Obstacles should be a part of your plan for success, just don't make them your focus. When you are experiencing fear, and you will, don't let it run your life. Fear is just one of those obstacles to overcome. The fear of taking a risk has killed many opportunities. In order to venture out and accomplish more, it involves taking risks and facing your fears. So, don't allow your fear to debilitate you. Those who risk little, grow little—and earn little. If you have truly made a decision to have more, you will face the risks and your fears at all costs, and you will grow as a result, both personally as well as financially.

There are twelve success principles in this book, but a principle is not an action step you take once and then it's done. A principle is an ongoing guideline for living. As you work with these principles, you will realize more and more that they are each designed to help you to access your own inner wisdom and strength, so that you can move with greater clarity and ease toward your goals and dreams. If you work with the principles and make them a part of daily life, they will work for you in creating the results you desire.

My hope is that you will use the principles in this book, like thousands of others have, to create a life for yourself that is adventurous instead of safe, prosperous instead of mediocre, and uncommon instead of common. May it be a life that is, in every way, *rich!* I would love to meet you one day on life's red carpet and celebrate your success story!

About the Author

Jim Britt, entrepreneur, author, speaker, and peak-performance specialist, is a seasoned organizational executive, a noted success counselor, and an internationally recognized leader in the field of personal-empowerment and business training. His background includes all levels of business experience, research, and application. Over the past thirty years, Jim has founded many successful ventures that range from real estate development to owning and operating a chain of nationwide health clinics. As a human behavior specialist for hundreds of prestigious companies, Jim has also helped countless employees reach their true potential, both professionally and personally.

Early in Jim's career, he served as President of Dr. Denis Waitley's Psychology of Winning, Vice President of Jim Rohn's Adventures in Achievement, and President of Dr. Maxwell Maltz's Psycho Cybernetics, International in order to gain experience in the speaking arena.

As a motivational speaker, Jim Britt is also the man who gave Tony Robbins his first real job—a job that inspired Tony to go out on his own and gain the financial freedom Jim had promised.

Throughout the United States, Canada, and Europe, Jim has shared his business-success principles and life-enhancing realizations with over one million people from all walks of life. He is more than aware of the personal challenges everyone faces—in business and other areas of life—and is dedicated to helping his audience make adaptive changes for a sustainable future.

Index

V

W